INTRODUCTION TO

Business Technologies

Alicen B. Flosi

Kendall Hunt
publishing company

Cover image © Shutterstock, Inc.

Kendall Hunt
publishing company

www.kendallhunt.com
Send all inquiries to:
4050 Westmark Drive
Dubuque, IA 52004-1840

Copyright © 2010 by Kendall Hunt Publishing Company

ISBN 978-0-7575-7240-1

Printed in the United States of America
10 9 8 7 6 5 4 3 2 1

Contents ☐☐☐

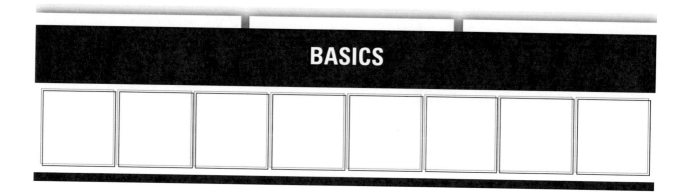

STUDENT LEARNING OUTCOMES

After successfully completing this chapter, students will be able to:

1. Demonstrate the basic functions of Windows XP including: saving, copying, naming, renaming, and deleting files and folders.

2. Navigate the Internet to search for data using Boolean limiters/expanders.

3. Define and identify the most common and most dangerous technological security and privacy threats (including identity theft) and to be familiar with technological means of safely eliminating or neutralizing these threats.

How Do I...?

It's a challenge to put any technology information in written form because it becomes outdated two minutes later. However, printed books are still useful references. This book will serve as a source for basic information for many business technologies. It is written not only for business majors, but for everyone. It is hoped that you will be able to refer to this book for the next two minutes and for the next two years.

Technology isn't like math or reading, which need to be learned up front. Many people learn what they need to know about technology when they need to know it—when they buy a new MP4 Player or computer, or when they get a new job, hobby, or if they have a friend that urges them to use new technology Although there are some people who like to go through tutorials, most students prefer to have someone show them a few features to get them started and provide them with an easy-to-use reference for what they need to know rather than trying to cover everything possible up front. This book is written to facilitate that thinking—basic information will be presented to bring you up to speed, and after that you can use the book as a reference to find the information you need when you need it at school, at work, or at home.

Knowing that time is limited and information is not, unnecessary explanations and text have been eliminated from this text. What this means for you is that you will need to read the entire book and not be able to skim as much as you might have. You might also have to figure some things out for yourself or work with others. Once you learn the basics, you will be able to apply the knowledge in other situations without extensive training, not only for other software packages, but for technology in general.

If you prefer or need step-by-step instructions, there are many excellent free online tutorials that will get you caught up.

There are usually many ways to do the same thing on a computer or with software. This text will sometimes show you more than one way; use whichever you like. Unless it specifically states otherwise, use the left mouse button as opposed to the right.

Operating Systems

Computers need operating systems to work. Operating systems are the interface between the computer hardware (the physical components of the computer—the unit, the screen, the speaker, the mouse, etc.) and the user (you). The operating system manages and coordinates the activities. Some operating systems you might use or might have heard of are Mac OS X, Microsoft Windows, Linux, and Darwin. It's helpful to know a few basic features of operating systems to save you time and frustration. Here are some MS Windows features you should know:

a. How to find out which operating system you are using:

Start > Run > Type winver.exe > OK

b. How to find programs and start them:

Start > All Programs > Select the one you want

c. How to create a shortcut for a program on your desktop so you don't have to go through the steps listed in step b.

Start > All Programs > Select the one you want with your left mouse button and drag it to an open area of the desktop, release the mouse.

Or...

Right click on a blank area of the desktop > New > Shortcut > Browse to find the filename > Next > Type a name > Finish

d. How to change the background, desktop theme, date, time, and more:

Start > Control Panel > Select the category you need > Select the item and browse through the options, picking the one you like

e. How to delete software from your computer:

Start > Control Panel > Select the category you need > Select Add or Remove programs. Only delete ones you are sure you don't need (obviously). If you aren't familiar with a program, leave it there; many of them run behind the scenes to help your system operate.

f. The Control Panel is also where you can change printer settings, control the audio volume, and set the date and time.

✓ Project

Check and see which operating system you are using (if you don't know). Which is it?

1. _____

See what programs are installed on the computer you are working on. List three of them (MS Office is one; don't list the applications like Word and Excel separately).

2. _____

Change your desktop theme if you are working on a computer that allows this (some networks do not allow users to make changes). What did you change your background to?

3. _____

Find a Notepad or WordPad program on your computer. It may be under Accessories. These programs are very simple word processing programs that you can use to create a document that doesn't need lots of formatting or extra features. Type a paragraph about yourself—describe your family, friends, hobbies, job, etc. Make sure your paragraph doesn't have misspellings or grammatical errors and make sure it is "G-rated" or "family friendly." Save it as yourlastname.txt on your flashdrive using File > Save > Save it on your desktop. Which program did you use and what did you name the file?

4. _____

Saving Files

When you are saving a file the first time, you should designate where you want it to be—on your flash drive or on the computer's hard drive—under My Documents or on the desktop, or on the network. Try to use a name that tells you what the document is and, even though the computer will track the date, it can be helpful to put the date in the filename sometimes. Once you have saved a file and named it, you can press Ctrl s occasionally to replace the old saved version with the new version using the same name.

If you want to keep the original file and save your new, revised one under a different name, or make a backup copy in a different place, use Office Button > Save As.

Windows Explore

It's usually a good idea to develop an organization system for all of your files to save you time later. Right click on Start and select Explore (don't confuse this with Internet Explorer) to see how your computer is organized already. You will probably have the following:

- Desktop – this is the screen you see when you start to work on your computer (after you log in). You might be able to change the background or screensaver depending on the network you are working on. You can also save files to the desktop so that you can get to them quickly, but it can get pretty cluttered.

- My Documents – this is a folder set up for you where you can save things. Often it is the default, which means that things will be saved in here automatically if you don't select another option. If you click on the + next to My Documents, you'll see that there may already be some folders set up for you—My Pictures, My Music. You can also make folders of your own. To collapse the folder again, click on the -.

- My Computer – if you click on the +, you should find several folders. These include folders and files to help your computer run, and program files. Usually if you download new programs, they will create a folder here to put the program in. Also, notice that you can get to the other drives, like if you have a drive for outdated diskettes, a CD drive, a DVD drive, or a flash/USB drive.

- My Network Places – if you are on a school or work network, the administrator may set up some server space for you on the network. A network server is a computer that uses a network to deliver data and process requests to other computers. Servers may be in a different room, building, state, or country. They are often backed up regularly and have good security, so it can become a good habit to keep copies of files on the network.

- Recycle Bin – this is where you throw things away when you don't need them anymore

- If you are selecting files, for example to recycle, you can click on them and drag them across to the recycle bin. But, to save time, you can also select more than one. Click on the first one > press and hold the Ctrl key > Click on the others (only the ones you selected should be highlighted; the files in between should not be highlighted) > Drag where ever you want.

- Notice that there are different Views in Explore. Selecting the Details view will allow you to see the filename, file size, file type, and the date it was last modified. The thumbnail view can be good for pictures.

a. How to set up folders to organize your files better:

Right click on Start > Select Explore > Select the location where you want the new folder, i.e. Desktop > File > New > Folder

A new folder will be set up and the cursor will be waiting for you to give it a name. Name it whatever you like.

b. How to copy files using Explore:

Right Click on Start > Select Explore > Select the file you want to copy by clicking with the left mouse button. Hold the mouse button down, move to the new location, and release your finger when the correct location is highlighted.

c. How to rename files using Explore:

Usually right clicking on a file will bring up several options, one of them is often Rename.

Or, you can Right click on Start > Select Explore > Click once on the filename, move your mouse over a tiny bit and click again (double clicking in the same place will open the file; we don't want to do that right now). A box will appear around the filename and the cursor will be waiting for you to type the new name.

d. How to change your pointer scheme:

Start > Ctrl Panel > Printers and other hardware > Pointers. Select a scheme > Apply > OK.

e. How to take a screenshot:

There are often times when you actually need to show someone what the screen looks like, i.e., if you are preparing training materials, you might want to show participants what their screen should look like at different stages. To do this, click somewhere on the screen you want captured, press Ctrl and PrintScreen (don't confuse this with the Print option—PrintScreen is a key on your keyboard, usually located at the top right side of the keyboard).

If you want the background to show also, use Alt and PrintScreen.

On laptops, you usually use Shift or Function and PrintScreen.

It will seem like nothing happened, but it took a picture. Open a word processing or paint program MS Word, OpenOffice.org Writer, or similar software, and Paste. The screenshot will be inserted.

✓ Project

- Create a folder on your flash drive and name it MIS.

- Inside that folder, create five more folders for Miscellaneous, Word Processing, Spreadsheets, Databases, and Presentations.

- Move your yourlastname.txt file into the Miscellaneous folder.

- Rename the file yourfirstnameyourlastname.txt.

- Take a screenshot of your Explore screen so that all of the folders and the text file are visible.

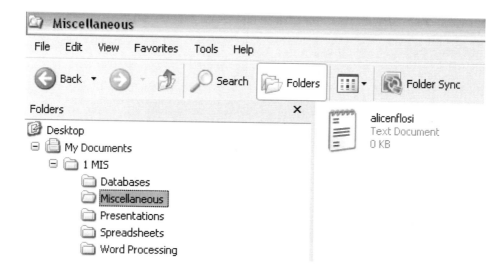

- Open a word processing program and Paste (Ctrl v) the screenshot. Save the file.

5. _____

Passwords

People have so many passwords, it's often difficult to remember them all and remember to follow good password rules. However, to the extent you can, it's good to:

- Use a password that is at least eight characters long.

- Use the following in your password:

  — At least one lowercase alpha character a–z

  — At least one uppercase alpha character A–Z

  — At least one numeric character 0–9

  — At least one special character (some might not be allowed) ` ! @ $ % ^ & * ( ) – _ = + [ ] ; : ' " , < . > / ?

Do not use the following in your password:

- Passwords like "asdf" or "1234"

- Names of pets or family members

- Student ID numbers, login IDs, phone numbers, or birthdays

It is better if you do not use actual words; however, you can modify them with characters or numbers, i.e., $allyM00re, gR8@day. You can check the strength of your password at sites such as http://www.microsoft.com/protect/yourself/password/checker.mspx.

> **Note:** *Passwords should be changed regularly, but do not write them on a sticky note and attach it to your computer because you are having trouble remembering them.*

Browsers

There are several browsers that you can use to access the Internet. These include Internet Explorer, Mozilla Browsers (Firefox, Netscape, and Camino 1), Opera, Safari, Chrome, and Konqueror. It's often a good idea to have two browsers installed on your computer in case one doesn't work with a Web site you are accessing or just to have for a backup.

Here are some browser features that can save you time and frustration:

1. Ctrl T – this will open a new Tab so that you can work on more than one thing at a time

2. Ctrl N – sometimes you need to open a whole new Window instead of just a new tab

3. History – it's a good idea to clear your history occasionally

4. Ctrl D – this will set up the page you are on as a favorite so that you can just select it from a list when you need it. Once you get several favorites, it's a good idea to organize them in folders, i.e., E-mail Folder if you have several e-mail accounts, Shopping Folder for your favorite shopping sites, etc.

5. Tools > Options > Startup (or something similar). You can change the home page, which is the first site the browser will go to when you open it.

It's often easier to use PDF files for sharing documents or controlling who can change information in a document. The most popular software for reading PDF files is Adobe Acrobat. The software can be found at www.adobe.com.

✔ Project

Install a second browser on your computer such as Mozilla Firefox, www.mozilla.com. Which two browsers are installed on your computer?

6. _____

Set up at least three bookmarks or favorites on one of the browsers. What are three of your favorites?

7. _____

Change your home page. What is your new home page?

8. _____

Experiment with some different browser features. Which feature that is not listed above will you use?

9. _____

Use the browser Help feature to read about Pop-Ups. What are Pop-Ups and how can you block them?

10. _____

Search Engines

With all of the information available on the Internet, it's important to know how to search. There are hundreds of search engines. Search engines are tools that are designed to find information on the Internet. Popular ones include Google, AltaVista, Yahoo!, HotBot, Excite, MSN, AllTheWeb, and Ask.

If you don't narrow your search down, you can get too many results that have nothing to do with what you are looking for. You can usually use plain English in your search, for example, "1950 Ford Mustang in good condition." You can also use the subcategories within the search engines. For example, in Google, you can search Images, Maps, News, Video, Shopping, YouTube, etc.

Another way to narrow your search is by using the Advanced Search that most search engines have. Advanced Search lets you enter exact words or phrases or omit certain words. For example, you can search for funny cartoons, but omit specific ones. You can also narrow searches down by using operators like NOT, a minus sign, AND, or sometimes by using features such as quotations around your search words. A * in a search will instruct the search engine to use that as a wildcard; for example, entertain* would find anything beginning with entertain—entertainment, entertainer, entertaining, entertains, etc.

All of the search engines have suggestions and tips for effective searches.

Tips:

- Don't give out or post personal information on the Internet.
- Have a second e-mail account for "junk e-mail" (open one at a free e-mail site—Gmail, Yahoo, Hotmail, etc.)
- Only download software from trusted sites.

✔ *Project*

Use any two search engines to search for a phrase (anything more than one word long), i.e., artificial intelligence. See how many results you received in each search engine and review a few of them to see if they are relevant. Which two search engines did you use and which had the best results?

11. _____

Now use the Advanced Search feature or an operator to see if you can narrow your search down, i.e., artificial not intelligence. Did you find fewer results? Did using Advanced Search or operators help?

12. _____

Now try a few more search engines. Hint: there are many you've never heard of. Search for "search engines" on a search engine to see what other ones are available. Which is your favorite?

13. _____

Search the Internet for free online tutorials for the software you are interested in learning. If you don't have a preference, search for online training about Windows Vista or Microsoft Windows. Briefly try out a few of the tutorials. Which online training seemed easiest to use and gave you the most information?

14. _____

Search the Internet for job-posting sites where you can post your resumes. Did any of these impress you? Were you unsure of the credibility or security of any sites? Which was your favorite?

15. _____

Other Internet Features

There isn't enough time or space to familiarize you with everything on the Internet, but here are some interesting features.

- Mapping sites can be useful even if you have a GPS; just remember they may not be 100 percent accurate due to traffic changes, construction, or incomplete information. Some common mapping sites are MSN, Google mapping, and MapQuest.

- If you are curious or suspicious about a Web site, you can copy the URL (Web address) into http://samspade.org.

- Recognizing fakes requires you to be careful. If you are suspicious, there are sites that you can use to verify claims and information. For example, if you suspect you received a fraudulent e-mail claiming to be from E-bay or PayPal, you can forward it to spoof@ebay.com or spoof@paypal.com.

- The best advice is to not forward e-mails to all of your friends and family if they sound too good or too crazy to be true. You can verify many of these at www.snopes.com or www.truthorfiction.com.

.AERO	Reserved for members of the air-transport industry
.BIZ	Restricted for Business
.INFO	Generic top-level domain
.JOBS	Reserved for human resource managers
.MIL	Reserved exclusively for the US Military
.MUSEUM	Reserved for museums
.NAME	Reserved for individuals
.ORG	Charitable or not-for-profit organizations

Besides the common domains you know, e.g., .com, .edu, and .gov, there are many more. Most of them are reserved for countries. You can see a list of these domains at http://www.iana.org/domains/root/db/. Here are a few of the less common domains.

Software Programs

Best Price Ever! Free!—open source software is publicly available for free. Companies that develop open source software make their source code available so that the design can be improved. Some examples of open source software are OpenOffice.org Suite, mysql.com (database), Dia found at live.gnome.org (drawing software), NVU.com (Web authoring system), and gimp.org (image editing, photo retouching). The Linux operating system is also open source. If you download open source software, monetary donations are welcome, of course, but not mandatory.

Downloading Software – It is still possible to buy most software on a CD or DVD, but if you have a fast Internet connection, it can be much easier to download the software as long as it is from a reliable source. When downloading software, follow the directions. A zip file will often be installed on your desktop. Once that is done, usually double clicking on the icon will start the installation. If you are unfamiliar with the software, select the standard installation instead of the custom installation, which will ask you to make selections you may not be familiar with.

Software Suites

Software Suites – A software suite is a collection of software, usually with a common interface that works together. For example, application software suites often include word processing, spreadsheet, presentation, and database applications. Some of the most common suites are Microsoft Office, Corel WordPerfect Office, Apple iWork, Lotus, and OpenOffice.org. OpenOffice.org is free open source software that is so similar to MS Office that the transition from one to the other is usually very easy.

Application software is software that is designed to help the user with a specific task. For example, word processing software assists the user in creating documents such as letters, reports, and agendas. The word processing software included in MS Office is MS Word. The word processing software included in OpenOffice is OpenOffice.org Writer.

The application software that is used with documents that require processing lots of numbers is spreadsheet software. It can be used for budgets, accounting statements, price lists, inventory lists, and loan documents. In MS Office, the spreadsheet software is MS Excel. In OpenOffice, it is OpenOffice.org Calc.

Two other types of application software that are often included in Suites are presentation software (for making slideshows and other types of presentations) and databases (for keeping track of data such as inventory lists, customer information, and employee information). MS Office has PowerPoint presentation software and Access database software. OpenOffice.org has OpenOffice.org Impress presentation software and OpenOffice.org Base database software.

Online software has become more popular due to the ability to access files anywhere and collaborate on files easily. Popular online software includes Google docs, zoho.com, and thinkfree.com.

 Project

Download and install openoffice.org from their Web site. How long did it take? Did you run into any problems?

16. _____

Enterprise Software

Enterprise software is used throughout a company to integrate all parts of the business. For example, the HR department can use the ERP software to keep track of employee addresses and basic information, and the Payroll office can also use it to keep track of employee pay data. Once the employee's name and address are entered into the enterprise system by HR, it will be accessible to the Payroll office.

There are many different enterprise software systems. Many are customized to the industry, i.e., hospitals, banks, certain manufacturing industries, but also most enterprise software is produced so that it has the basic business functions and then can be adapted to a specific organization. One of the most common enterprise systems is SAP.

Chapter 5 discusses ERP software in greater detail.

Course Management Software

Course Management Software allows instructors and students to have better communication and easier management of paperwork, grades, and lectures. One common course management system is Blackboard. Most course management systems have discussion boards, assignment submission, chat rooms, posting of lecture

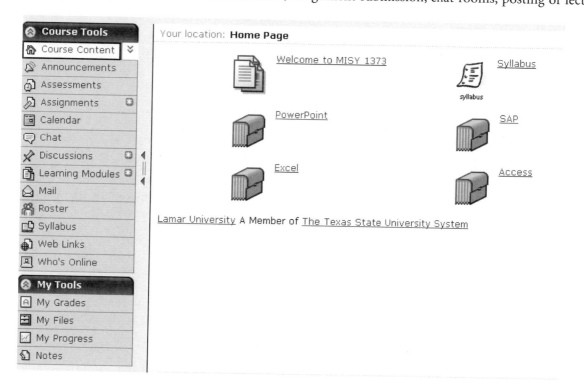

notes or other class materials, e-mail, and testing. Students should check the course management software often so they don't miss e-mails or announcements.

The following image shows a course in Blackboard. Notice the menu options along the right hand side. Typically you can click on each of these to see what they contain. Instructors can limit your access to materials, so if they don't want you to see something, it won't be there.

Your instructors select which categories will be used in your class; you may only see a few of them. Most of the categories are easy to understand, but here is a brief description of a few of them:

- Course Content – this is your home page (the page in the diagram)

- Announcements – if there is an announcement from the instructor, you might find it here. Announcements can also be set up to pop-up automatically when you login. Blackboard might also post announcements, for example, making you aware of changes to the software.

- Assessments – this is where your instructor will place quizzes and tests

- Assignments – assignments can be posted here, for example, as an Adobe file. You will also hand in your assignments here, the same way you do an attachment in an e-mail.

- Calendar – your instructor might post due dates on the calendar as an easy reminder for students

- Chat – chats can be set up with the instructor, and students can also chat when the instructor isn't present. This can be a very helpful feature for team projects.

- Discussions – this is a posting board for the instructor and students. Many instructors have students post journal article reviews here so that other students can comment and read them. It can also be a great place to post questions for other students to answer if there is something you are unclear about.

- Learning modules – lectures, slideshows, and other class information can be placed here for students to access. Some lectures for online classes might include audio, so make sure you check to see if your speakers need to be on.

- Mail – e-mail, of course. Some systems like Blackboard don't give you an e-mail address; they just work within the Blackboard system. This is a great location to communicate with other students because you can select their name off of a list to e-mail them. Instructors can also e-mail all students easily.

- Syllabus – the syllabus will probably be posted here

- Who's online – if you are working online and need help, you can check this to see if any other students or the instructor are online. If they are, you can send them a message to see if they want to chat. Don't get your feelings hurt if they don't reply; sometimes they are working on something else or have left the room to get a Dr. Pepper and they don't see the invitation.

- My grades – obvious. Although, just a comment—sometimes grades aren't posted until all assignments have been turned in or graded. The instructor can control when grades are released. After an appropriate amount of time has passed, you can politely check with your instructor—sometimes we forget to make grades visible.

Also, as in the image, your instructor can place items on the Home Page so you can access them from there without using the side menus.

Tip: *Blackboard seems to work best with Firefox. If you have problems logging in, check to make sure pop-ups are allowed.*

Project

Post the URL (Web address) of one of your favorite Web sites on the discussion board under the appropriate link.

17. _____

Security

Security usually isn't a concern until it's breached. Obviously, it's necessary to make your computer secure before there are any problems. This includes using a reliable firewall and anti-virus program. Check often for updates for your operating system and security software. New viruses are created every minute. The best way to remember to check your system is to set the software to automatically update when the computer isn't in use, for example, three times a week at 2:00 A.M.

You can purchase software with your computer or online. There are many excellent Internet security programs including www.avast.com, www.avg.com, www.spybot.info/en/index.html, www.lavasoft.com, www.pctools.com/free-antivirus, www.malwarebytes.org, www.comodo.com, and www.javacoolsoftware.com. The important thing when selecting security software is to read professional reviews and see how often it is updated.

✔ *Project*

Either run the virus software that is installed on your computer or run Housecall from http://housecall.trendmicro.com/. What software did you use and what were the results?

18. _____

Computer Maintenance

If not maintained regularly, your computer can become sluggish and will run much slower than it needs to. To keep your computer running better, use scan disk and defrag regularly. This will organize the files and erase unneeded files. The easiest way to perform regular maintenance on your computer is to set it to perform the functions itself at regular intervals when the computer isn't in use.

In addition:

- Use a UPS (uninterruptible power source), which will save your computer from power outages and electrical spikes.

- Shut your computer down with Start > Turn off computer > Shut down instead of using the power switch. This will prevent many problems.

- Do not unplug printers, keyboards, etc., while the power is on.

- Remove programs from the startup so that the computer will work faster. If they load during startup, they are running in the background while you are working. You can do this yourself or use a program like www.ccleaner.com to help.

- Keep software updated; updates will fix known problems and help your software run more smoothly.

Project

These might take awhile if you haven't been doing them regularly. If you don't have a computer that you can use, work with a partner. Run Disk Cleanup. Start > All Programs > Accessories > System Tools > Disk Cleanup. What were the results and how long did it take (approximately)?

19. _____

If you don't have a computer that you can use, work with a partner. Run Disk Fragmenter. Start > All Programs > Accessories > System Tools > Disk Fragmenter. What were the results and how long did it take (approximately)?

20. _____

> **Backups!!** *This is a very important tip because the first time you forget to do it will be the night you lose three hours work and have to cancel a night out with your friends. Save often and backup your work. Backups need to be saved in a different place than your original; save on your computer and a flash drive, or e-mail it to yourself. Just make sure the backup worked, especially if you are working on a school network or in a public library or Internet café where you can't save to the computer.*

Basic Shortcuts and Tips

Learning some shortcuts and tips can save time and frustration. Many of them work whether you are on the Internet or working in a specific software package.

- Undoing what you just did (and often what you did before that and before that and before that)... – Ctrl z

- Copy – use the mouse to select the item to be copied and press Ctrl c

- Cut – this is used to move something instead of simply copying it; use the mouse to select the item to be moved and press Ctrl x

- Paste – after copying or cutting something, click on the location you want it copied to and press Ctrl v

- Insert Key – pressing this will cause your entry to replace whatever is already entered instead of inserting it and moving everything over.

- Saving Easily – Ctrl s

- Help – F1

- Quit program – Alt F4

- Redoing an action – Ctrl y

- Browsing – if you need to attach a file or find one, you can browse for it by clicking on folders to find it. If you need to go back because it's not where you thought, you don't have to start over; just click on the back arrow or go up on the document path.

STUDENT LEARNING OUTCOMES

After successfully completing this chapter, students will be able to:

1. Demonstrate basic computer functions including communication through electronic methods such as e-mail, bulletin or discussion boards, and other means of asynchronous and synchronous communication through tools such as Blackboard.

2. Demonstrate ability to function as a contributing team member.

Communication

People are communicating more than ever. This is a good thing as long as we are good communicators. Unfortunately, we aren't all good communicators, and most of us think we are better than we really are.

Remember to *be careful about what you say or write*; it can't be undone, and often it can be distributed to everyone you know in seconds, even if you think you deleted it. One day, a prospective employer might look at your Facebook page, or a current employer might need to review past e-mails sent from company computers. If it's not something you feel comfortable showing up on everyone's e-mail or youTube, better not say it, text it or video it.

✔ *Project*

Search the Internet for an example of miscommunication or an example of information getting to the wrong people. What was the most interesting situation you found or your favorite finding?

1. _____

Proofreading and Business English

In your college career, hopefully you will take a Business Communications class that will help you with the wording of letters, e-mails, presentations, resumes, and other kinds of business communication. For this class, we are mainly interested in learning how to use technology in preparing those business communications.

This doesn't mean that the content can be extremely casual or that grammar and spelling aren't important. Proofread everything carefully before you hit send, post, or print. If you have weak proofreading skills, ask someone else to proof your work first. And remember, the spelling and grammar checks on software are helpful but they don't catch everything. They think this sentence is correct: The see was ruff and the water was clear. Until software becomes more advanced, it won't know whether you mean 'your' or 'you're.'

 ## Project

Search the Internet for an example of incorrect grammar or misspelled words. What was your favorite finding?

2. _____

Sometimes people selling items on online auctions, like e-Bay, misspell something in their description; this can be a great way to find a good deal because other buyers might not see it. This is so common there are even software tools designed to help you find these misspellings. Search e-Bay for an item, but misspell it (using a possible misspelling, e.g., moniter instead of monitor). What was your favorite finding?

3. _____

Social Networks

Social networks were created to keep people in touch with each other, but they have become more than that as businesses use them to attract and keep customers. There are many, including Facebook, MySpace, Bebo, and Classmates. Search for 'social networks'—you'll find many that you didn't know existed.

These sites are meant to be casual, so there aren't many rules. The main rule is: remember that you cannot control who has access, even when you limit accessibility to friends. Use these sites carefully and wisely.

Here is some information on networking sites you may have heard of:

- Plaxo was started by Napster co-founder, Sean Parker, Minh Nguyen and two Stanford engineering students, Todd Masonis and Cameron Ring. It is used for automatic updating of contact information.

- Twitter is a free networking site that allows members to send short messages (tweets) to people who have signed up to receive them (followers). Musicians and actors use Twitter to keep in touch with fans. Businesses are now beginning to use Twitter also.

For many people, activity is high at the beginning, but lessens as they realize the time commitment or become less interested.

Professional Networks

To maintain a more professional presence on the Internet, many turn to professional networks such as LinkedIn. These allow you to network with other people in your field, building a base of professionals for business needs such as finding potential clients, sharing contacts and knowledge, and listing business information. These sites are also useful for school alumni groups and finding and posting job openings.

Other professional networks are: Yorz, Ecademy, Ryze, and Xing.

 ## Project

Talk to three people. What social and professional networking sites have they heard of? Which sites do they use, if any? Which do you use? List three advantages and three disadvantages of social/professional networks.

4. _____

Blogs and Discussion Boards

Of course, there are lots of other ways to communicate.

- Blogs allow users to post entries about any topic they choose. The topic may be themselves, or the blog may be set up to discuss a certain topic like gardening.

- Discussion boards allow users to carry on an online discussion.

- Texting, of course, allows users to send brief messages over cellular networks. These are not only used in personal situations, but also in the work environment. For example, texting can be a quick way to send an important work message to someone in a meeting. However, in the work environment, much of the texting shorthand is not allowed. KNIM? (That stands for "Know what I mean?" If you didn't know that, you might want to check out http://www.webopedia.com/quick_ref/textmessageabbreviations.asp.)

- E-mailing, of course, allows you to send electronic mail. There are some business etiquette rules for e-mails: use of courtesy, use of more direct language than formal written communication, etc. Four important notes:
  — Use a businesslike e-mail address for your resume. You might want to open a new e-mail account if your current one is hotstuff@.com or 2beers2many@.com.
  — Be careful who you copy on e-mails and when using 'Reply All.' Many problems have been caused by accidentally sending an e-mail to someone.
  — The BCC (blind courtesy copy) will send a copy to the person, but other recipients will not know that person got a copy. This can be useful for documenting situations or creating a paper trail.
  — Never use your work e-mail for personal e-mails and don't send colleagues personal e-mails, no matter how sure you are that they won't be offended. People have lost jobs over innocent e-mails sent through the work e-mail system.

- Videos allow companies and individuals to share information. These are not limited to YouTube. Online videos have become more popular as connection speeds have improved. Of course, be careful about what you post on YouTube and similar sites, but also become aware of the helpful information that is available.

- Podcasts are multimedia files that can be downloaded to mobile devices or computers. Your instructor might make a podcast of a lecture.

- A wiki is a site that allows users to easily create and edit the content of a website. Wikis are often used to create community websites and for note taking. Wikipedia, a collaborative encyclopedia, is one of the best-known wikis.

✔ *Project*

Find a blog where customers are discussing a product or service (e.g., hotel, appliance, shoe, etc.). What was the product or service? Were a majority of the comments positive or negative?

5. _____

Log into the course management software used by your class and post a paragraph or two about yourself on the discussion board. Remember everyone in the class will read these, so keep them "family-friendly." Read some of the other students' postings.

What was one thing that you remember reading about someone and whose posting was it?

6. _____

Who do you think you have the most in common with? Why?

7. _____

Calendars

Calendars have become vital planning tools now that we have the capability to link our calendars with other peoples. If bosses want to schedule meetings, they can check calendars of the people that should attend and select a time everyone is available. Notices can automatically be sent to you and to anyone else who needs the information. The MS Outlook calendar and Google's calendar programs are both popular shared calendar software. They also allow you to sync your calendar with a mobile device.

Some of the other features are the ability to import other calendars easily, such as importing U.S. holidays into your calendar. Also, recurring appointments can easily be set up. For example, a class you will attend every Monday evening from 8:00 to 9:00 for the next 12 weeks only has to be set up once.

The Blackboard calendar makes it easy for instructors to distribute due dates to all students.

 *Project*

Set up a Gmail account, then go to calendar.google.com and create a calendar for yourself for at least a couple of months. Import the US holidays and add a few special university events (Spring Break, etc.) Add at least five personal events (work schedule, birthdays, etc.) Notice some of the other features available: sharing, viewing by day or week or month, creating task lists, and printing. When you complete your calendar, with the month view on the screen, take a screenshot.

8. The screenshot is Project 8. You instructor will advise you on submission instructions.

Meetings

You may not have had jobs where you attended meetings yet, but you probably will. Many meetings are held online to save time and money. There are different options for online meetings, including video, audio, screen display, desktop sharing, and web conferencing. Common meeting software are: MS Live Meeting, WebEx, and Adobe Acrobat Connect. Second Life is a free 3D virtual world where users can socialize, connect, and create using voice and text chat. In Second Life, users create an avatar. Facebook uses a similar idea for Farm Town, which allows you to create and manage a farm, hiring others from Facebook and working on their farms.

 Project

Experiment with Second Life, Farm Town, or another free, safe online community; talk to friends who have used either one; or research an online community. What are some of the benefits and disadvantages of these as a communication method?

9. _____

Research

There is a great deal of information on the Internet, but it isn't always accurate or acceptable for research. For many situations, you will need to research scholarly or peer-reviewed articles – these are ones that have been reviewed by someone knowledgeable on the topic before they are published. It's important to know how to find scholarly or peer-reviewed articles in the university library.

 Project

Using the university library site, find a business article on any technology topic you are interested in (e.g., virtual reality, robotics, GPS). Limit your search to full-text (the entire article, not just the abstract), academic, or peer-reviewed articles published after 1/1/2007.

Select an article that interests you to read. Post a one-paragraph summary of the article, the bibliographical information, and a link to the article on the discussion board and type the name of the article for Project 10.

10. _____

chapter 3

SOFTWARE TIPS

STUDENT LEARNING OUTCOMES

After successfully completing this chapter, students will be able to:

1. Demonstrate the ability to utilize software shortcuts to perform basic functions such as copying and saving data.

Software developers have realized that customers are happier if many features are similar in different software packages. This makes it easier for people to learn one system and easily adapt to a different one.

Open MS Word so that you can experiment with some of these features.

Shortcuts

The following are MS Office features and shortcuts. Many of these work in a variety of software programs:

Ctrl z – undo	Ctrl y – redo	Ctrl s – save
Ctrl c – copy	Ctrl p – print	F7 – check spelling
Ctrl x – cut	Ctrl o – open	Ctrl n – new file
Ctrl v – paste	Ctrl f – find text	Ctrl h – find/replace
Ctrl w – close window	Ctrl End – move to the end of the document	Ctrl Home – move to beginning of document
Ctrl g – go to	F1 – Help	Ctrl k – hyperlink
Ctrl a – select all	Home – move to beginning of the line	End – move to the end of the line

Also, notice that there are keys for Page Up and Page Down. And that you can zoom (make the text appear larger or smaller) using the zoom slider at the bottom right corner. Note that the text is not actually larger; it just appears that way on the screen.

If you click on the Office Button (circle in the top left corner), you will see options for opening, saving, printing, etc.

In this example, shortcuts are also set up on the Quick Access Toolbar (right next to the Office Button) for saving, undoing, printing, print preview, etc. If you want to set up shortcuts, click on the arrow and select the ones you want.

✓ Project 1

Add whichever shortcuts you like on the Quick Access Toolbar and take a screenshot of it.

Dialog Box

Other chapters will cover some of the features in the tabs and groups, but notice the dialog box launcher next to the Clipboard group, Font group, the Paragraph group, and the Styles group. If a group has this arrow, this means that there are more choices available.

Help!

Of course, the __ on the top right minimizes the screen, the box next to it will maximize or restore down, and the X closes the software. The ? takes you to MS Office online help. This is an easy way to find out how to use a software feature.

AutoRecover

One nice feature in MS Office is the ability to use AutoRecover . This can save you a lot of time and aggravation if the power goes off while you are working on something or if you lose a file for some reason. If AutoRecover is turned on (Office Button > Options > Save > Set the settings however you like), your file can be recovered when you get back into the software. It might be missing a few of the changes you made after the last time it automatically saved it, but it will still be better than recreating the entire file.

Document Inspector

If you want to make sure your document doesn't have any hidden text, like revisions, comments, or personal information about the author, you can run the document inspector. To run the document inspector, click on the Office Button, > Prepare > Inspect Document > Select the type of content you want to be inspected > Inspect > Review the results and remove the ones you want deleted. Note: Hidden content that is removed might not be recoverable, even using Undo.

AutoCorrect

MS Office can automatically correct spelling and grammar if you want it to, or you can have it identify possible errors so that you can correct them. Also, if there is a word you typically misspell, you can add it to autocorrect. Office Button > Options (at the bottom) > Proofing > On the AutoCorrect Options > AutoCorrect tab, make sure the Replace Text as You Type box is selected > In the Replace box, type a word you often misspell > In the With box, type the correct spelling of the word > Add.

✔ Project 2

Use AutoCorrect to set up a word that you often misspell. Take a screenshot of the setup screen.

Overtype or Insert

Usually when you type, you want to insert text instead of typing over text. However, if you want to type over text and replace it with what you are typing, you can use the overtype option instead of deleting and then inserting. The overtype option might be turned on. To see if it is, type a few words in MS Word and then click between two words to type a word between them. For example, type "What a day!" Then, click before "day" and type "fantastic". The text should move over as you insert the word. Now, press the Insert key (to toggle it to overtype) and click before the "f" in "fantastic" and type "wonderful". If overtype is on, it will replace fantastic with wonderful.

To turn on overtype, click on Office Button > Options > Advanced > Under Edition Options, select the Use Overtype Mode box (you can turn it off by clearing the Use Overtype Mode box).

WORD PROCESSING SOFTWARE

STUDENT LEARNING OUTCOMES

After successfully completing this chapter, students will be able to:

1. Create basic word processing documents such as newsletters, letters, and reports.

2. Demonstrate the use of word processing features to emphasize key points, catch the reader's attention, and improve a document's appearance.

Usually if you are entering text, you will use word processing software. For example, you may be preparing a letter, report, or memo. Popular word processing software includes MS Word, OpenOffice Doc, and Google Docs.

Templates

Most software has predesigned templates that will save you some time. The ones in MS Word often even give suggestions for the text. For example, the thank you letter for customers provides basic language and then places where you can insert specific text to customize it. Usually, however, it is better to write letters from scratch; a business communications course can help you learn how to write effective letters, speeches, resumes, reports, etc.

Take a minute to look at some of the free templates available in MS Word:

Office Button > New > Scroll through the options at the left. There are some installed and many more available online.

Open any of the letter templates. Notice that most of these can help you make sure you have the required information, such as inside address and salutation, and that it is in the right place. Just remember, if you aren't going to enter text in one of the placeholders, delete it!

Blank Document

You can create a document on a blank page by:

• Office Button > New > Blank Document

or

• Ctrl N

or

- Set up the New icon on your Quick Access Toolbar at the top left.

✔ *Practice*

- Open a new blank document.

Entering Data in MS Word

Entering data in Word simply requires the ability to type, whether you use one finger or ten. Don't press Enter when you get to the end of a line; the software will take you down to the next line when needed.

Sometimes people want to type farther down a page; for example, they type a paragraph and then want a blank area before the next paragraph. You cannot use the arrow keys to move down if there is nothing to move down to. There are several ways to do this; for now, you can use the Enter key to add some blank lines if you want to type lower on the page.

Word Count and Page Information

As you type, the software will give you some information.

- On the bottom left of the screen, it will tell you what page you are on and the total number of pages.
- It will also tell you the number of words.

Views

Also notice at the bottom of the screen that there are controls for how the document looks ON THE SCREEN, not on paper. For example, you can:

- Slide the indicator to zoom in or out.
- Change the views to:
  — Print layout – this is the one we usually use.
  — Full Screen reading (to get out of this, click on X Close in the top right corner of the screen)
  — Web layout
  — Outline or draft

✔ *Practice*

- Type at least two paragraphs, with a total word count of at least 200 words, about anything you like—your life, your job, your dreams, a favorite movie or TV show, etc. This will give you a document to work with.
- Change the views.
- Press Enter a few times at the end of one of your paragraphs to open up some blank space.

Saving Files

To save a file you have the same two basic options:

1. Option 1 – Save. Use this if you have already named and saved the file and you want to replace the original with the one you are working on. While you are working on a file that you haven't saved, it will be given a generic name like Document 1.

i) Office Button > Save

ii) Or Ctrl S

iii) Or use Save icon on the quick access toolbar

2. Option 2 – Save As. Use this if you are working on a file and you want to keep the original and save the version you are working on under a different name or in a different location.

i) Office Button > Save As

It's usually a good idea to organize your files by using folders. If you were using a file cabinet, you wouldn't just put all of the papers in one big drawer; you would separate them with folders so things are easier to find. Setting up a folder in MS Word is easy; you don't even have to have it created ahead of time.

First, you will need to make sure where your folder and file will be saved: under My Documents, on the desktop, on a flash drive (USB), etc. If you click on the arrow, you will get a drop down list of choices. The following screenshot is pointing to the flash drive, which is drive E on this computer. If you don't designate the location, it may be hard to find your file later.

The folder icon shown on the right of the screen in the following screenshot is for setting up a new folder. Just click on it and name your folder. You can also use Alt 4.

✓ Practice

- Create a folder on your desktop or flash drive called Word Processing.

- Save your paragraph in that folder under any name you choose, but select a name that will tell you what the file is; for example, My Trip to Hawaii or My Job or Practicing Word Processing.

Notice that your file is still open even though you've saved it. It's a good idea to save occasionally (Ctrl S) just in case the power goes off or something happens.

Note: *By selecting a different option under Save as: you can also save files as Web pages to be opened with a browser or as PDF files.*

Selecting Text

There are several ways to select text in MS Word using the mouse or keyboard. Here are some of the most common methods.

- To select everything in your document
  - — Go to Select (far right side of Home tab) and Select All
  - — Or Ctrl A
- To select any amount of text – use the mouse by clicking at the beginning of the text you are selecting, holding the mouse button down and dragging to the end of the selected text and lifting your finger
- To select a word – click twice anywhere in the word
- To select a line – move the cursor to the left of the line until it is an arrow, then click
- To select a sentence – hold down Ctrl and click anywhere in the sentence
- To select a paragraph – click three times anywhere in the paragraph
- To select text that is not right next to each other – select the text in the first location, hold down Ctrl, and select the rest of the text

✔ Practice

- MS Word Help lists methods for selecting single characters, words, lines, and paragraphs. Use MS Help (click on the ? in the top right corner and search for select text) to find out how to select a paragraph from its end to its beginning using the keyboard.
- Using the mouse, select one sentence from the middle of your paragraph.
- Select one word in your paragraph.
- Select one paragraph.

Deleting

There are a few methods for deleting text:

- You can move your curser before the text you want to delete and press Delete to delete the text to the right of the cursor.
- You can use the Backspace key to delete text to the left of the curser.
- You can select the text with the mouse and press the Delete key.
- Pressing Ctrl backspace will delete one word to the left.
- Pressing Ctrl delete will delete one word to the right.

Formatting

Many formatting options are on the Home tab. You can set formatting instructions before you type the text or after you type it.

The Clipboard allows you to:

- Cut (either to move or delete) a selection or Ctrl x
- Copy or Ctrl c
- Paste or Ctrl v
- Format paint (paintbrush) or Ctrl Shift c

You can also move text by selecting it, clicking on it, and dragging it (holding the mouse button down) to its new location.

✔ *Practice*

- Select a word and cut it out, then select another location to move it to (Ctrl x, Ctrl v).
- Select a sentence and copy it to another location (Ctrl c, Ctrl v).
- Let's undo those actions – press Ctrl z a couple of times until your document is back to normal. If you go too far, you can always redo it with Ctrl y.

Font

Most of the Font selections are fairly easy to understand. And MS Word allows you to see what your changes will look like if you select some text before making the selection.

- Font face – there a many fonts installed with the software. Remember to select ones that are easy to read. Clicking on the arrow shows all of the available fonts.
- The font size arrow allows you to select what size you want the font to be.
- The icons with the two capital A's also control the font. Selecting text and then clicking on the larger A increases the font size. Selecting text and then clicking on the smaller A decreases the font size.
- If you don't like the way text is formatted, you can select the text and click on the 🔲 icon next to the font size icons and it will take away the formatting and make it plain text.

The second row in the Font Group has icons for:

- Bold – you can also use Ctrl b
- Italics – you can also use Ctrl i
- Underlining – you can also use Ctrl u. If you click on the arrow next to the underline icon, you'll see other choices for <u>underlining</u>.
- Strikethrough – if you are proofreading a document for someone and you think they should delete a word, but you want to leave it in so they can decide, you can strike through it.
- Subscript – H_2O. You can also use Ctrl =. This is a toggle button; it will keep formatting subscript until you click on it again to turn it off.
- Superscript – 1st. You can also use Ctrl Shift +. This is a toggle button; it will keep formatting superscript until you click on it again to turn it off.
- If you ever typed something and then wished it were all capitals or weren't all capitals, you'll like this **Aa**⁻ icon. It can convert text to lowercase, uppercase, sentence case (capitalize first word), capitalize each word (like in a title), or toggle case, which reverses the lowercase and uppercase.

- Text Highlighter – makes it look like you highlighted text with a pen. If you click the arrow next to it, you can select different colors to highlight with.
- Font Color – pretty self explanatory; there are lots of colors to pick from!

Now, let's talk about format painter, the paintbrush on the left. If you have formatting set up that you like and you want to quickly apply the same format to other text, you can select some of the formatted text, click on format painter, and then click on the text you want to be formatted the same way. Format painted will copy the format, but not the text.

✔ *Practice*

- Practice the following features on some of the text in your document:

• Font	• Font size
• Bold	• Italics
• Underlining	• Strikethrough
• Superscript	• Subscript
• Changing case	• Highlighting
• Font color	• Format painter

Your document might look a little messy now; you can undo those changes or leave a few of them and then save it.

Font format options are also available if you click on the arrow to the right of Font on the Home tab. As you can see, many of them are the same, but there are also additional choices.

Paragraph Formatting

Formatting paragraphs is easy also; you can set the format before you type the paragraph or type it first, select it, then apply the format.

Across the top row:

- The first icon is to add bullets, like the one used for this list. If you click the arrow next to it, you can change the appearance of the bullet to a circle, square, checkmark, arrow, etc. There are hundreds to pick from.

- The second icon is for numbering items. You can use standard numbers, numbers and letters, roman numerals, etc.

- The third icon is for multilevel lists. This can happen automatically, but you may want to select the style.

- The next icon increases the indention of the paragraph; it moves it over to the right a little.

- The next icon decreases the indention of the paragraph; it moves it over to the left a little.

- If you select a list or bulleted items and then click on the AZ icon, it will alphabetize the items.

- The ¶ displays formatting characters on the screen (but they won't print out). This can come in handy if you need to see what formatting is on the document, but it gets annoying if you have it set all of the time.

Note: Tips for bullets:

- When using bullets or lists, press enter at the end of each item.
    — If you need to move in a level for an item, use the Tab.
- If the next item should be back out at the left, use Shift Tab before you start typing it.

The second row of icons:

- Usually text is aligned at the left side of the paper; this is the first icon (Ctrl l) – left aligned.

- The next icon (Ctrl e) centers the text; you might use it for a title or if you are making a marketing brochure.

- The right align (Ctrl r) evens everything up on the right side and the left side is all uneven.

- The justify icon (Ctrl j) evens up both the left and the right sides; this is often used in printed books.

- Next is the line spacing icon. You can get very detailed with the choice on this icon. If you select 1, there will be no blank line between the text. If you select 2, there will be one blank line between the text. Or you can specify different spacing before or after paragraphs. Also, if you click on line spacing options, under line and page breaks, you can control whether you want to allow one single line to carry over to a new page or not or whether you want to allow hyphenation at the end of a line. This is necessary for formal reports.

- The paint bucket is for shading, which is really similar to the highlighting icon in the font group.

- The last icon in that group is for making borders. You can put a left border, right border, or border all the way around like in this paragraph. If you click on the arrow next to it, there are several more options.

Notice that you can also get to these features, and more, by clicking on the arrow next to Paragraph.

Take a minute to look at the options under Tabs in that dialog box.

Tabs are stops that you can set. For example, you might want a tab every five spaces. Or you can set up leaders like those that are used in a Table of Contents. Leaders are the dots or dashes that "lead" your eye over to the right.

1. Word Processing .... p. 2

2. Spreadsheets .... p. 5

✔ *Practice*

- Practice the following features on your paragraphs; you can add text if you like:

• Bullets	• Left align, right align, center
• Lists	• Change line spacing
• Multilevel lists (using tab and shift tab)	• Add shading
• Indention	• Add borders
• Sorting a list	

If your document is looking messy, put some of the text back to the way it was. You can keep the formatting you like.

Styles

Styles are fun and easy. They are preset styles that you can select. Often they give documents a more professional appearance. The word "Styles" above is in Heading Style. The text is in Intense Emphasis.

You can even change the styles. The options under that icon are Style Set, Colors, and Fonts. Be careful about using these; you can accidentally reformat your entire document. Clicking on the arrow next to Styles brings up the following dialog box:

Styles	▼ ×
Clear All	
acicollapsed1	a
Normal	¶
No Spacing	¶
Heading 1	¶a
Heading 2	¶a
Title	¶a
Subtitle	¶a
Subtle Emphasis	a
Emphasis	a
Intense Emphasis	a
Strong	a
Quote	¶a
Intense Quote	¶a
Subtle Reference	a
Intense Reference	a
Book Title	a
List Paragraph	¶

☐ Show Preview
☐ Disable Linked Styles

Options…

 Practice

- Practice using the Styles feature; change the style to find an attractive format.
- Save your file.

Find, Replace

We already looked at the Select button. Let's look at Find and Replace.

The Find option searches your entire document looking for the word you specify. You can go to Find Next to continue finding the word in the document.

Find and Replace

Find | Replace | Go To

Find what: [   ] ▼

[More >>]   Reading Highlight ▼   Find in ▼   Find Next   Cancel

The Replace option can save you a lot of time. For example, if you need to replace Aunt Sally with Uncle Marvin, you can have the software find each occurrence for you. Be careful, though. You might have to be more specific in your instructions; you wouldn't want it to replace every occurrence of men with women because it might replace the "men" in mental with women—womental, or the men in mention with women—womention. In these situations, you would not "Replace All"; you might want to use Find Next and Replace only for the ones that are appropriate.

To show some of the other options that are available, click on More on the Replace dialog box.

Find and Replace

Find | Replace | Go To

Find what: [Aunt Sally   ] ▼

Replace with: [Uncle Marvin   ] ▼

[<< Less]   Replace   Replace All   Find Next   Cancel

Search Options

Search: [All] ▼

☐ Match case   ☐ Match prefix
☐ Find whole words only   ☐ Match suffix
☐ Use wildcards
☐ Sounds like (English)   ☐ Ignore punctuation characters
☐ Find all word forms (English) ☐ Ignore white-space characters

Replace

[Format ▼] [Special ▼] [No Formatting]

✔ Practice

- Use Find/Replace on a word in your document that appears more than once.

Those are all of the features that are available on the Home tab.

Let's take a minute to look at the screen.

You can also set tabs and indents by using the settings at the end of the rulers. For example, by clicking on the setting on the left you can quickly change the left margin, indents, etc. Or, you can drag the markers on the ruler to set margins and tabs.

The Insert Tab

It's pretty easy to figure out what you would be doing with the Insert tab, but there are several features you may not be familiar with.

Pages

- Cover page – this is a template with several attractive cover pages to choose from. You just have to insert the title, author, etc., and, of course, delete any placeholders you don't need.

- Blank page – I think you can figure that out

- Page break – if the text isn't to the bottom of the page yet, and you want to go to the next page, click on this.

Table

Click on the arrow below the word Table. There are several ways to insert a table.

- If you move the cursor over the boxes, you can select the size table you want, i.e., 2 columns, 4 rows, etc.

- You can select Insert Table and use this dialog box.

- If you have some text that you want to convert to a table, you can select it and then click on Convert Text to Table.

- Also, you can use the Excel spreadsheet option; this opens up an Excel spreadsheet. As you enter the data in the spreadsheet, it will be entered on the Word document at the same time.

Notice that as you create a table in Word, two more tabs open up. These are for formatting your table.

With the Design tab you can:

- Include a total row

- Select a different table style

- Add shading

- Add borders with different widths or styles

With the Layout tab you can:

- Delete the table

- Insert rows and columns

- Merge cells, i.e. merging two cells to put in a title
- Change the cell size
- Align the text inside a cell – left, center, top of cell, bottom of cell, etc.
- Change the direction of the text

✓ *Practice*

- Insert the following table and practice formatting it with several of the features.

Chocolate chip	25 boxes
Oatmeal raisin	10 boxes
Sugar	6 boxes
M&M	12 boxes
Peanut butter	6 boxes

Sorting a Table

You can also sort a table quickly.

Select both columns and all five rows of your table. Then, in the Layout Tab under Table Tools, click on Sort. Notice it will sort by column 1 (which is what we want in this case) and there should be a checkmark in the box for No Header because we don't have column headings on our table.

Chocolate chip	25 boxes
M&M	12 boxes
Oatmeal raisin	10 boxes
Peanut butter	6 boxes
Sugar	6 boxes

Back to the Insert Tab – Picture

If you have an image or picture (usually ending in .gif, .jpeg, .jpg, or .png) you want to insert, click on Picture and find the file. Once you have the picture inserted, you'll notice that a new tab opens up for you to format the picture. You can add various borders, change the contrast, add a frame, add a shadow, make it three-dimensional, rotate it, and change other picture effects.

The picture can be placed within the text, at the left or right. You can move the picture around by using the arrow keys.

This picture uses "middle center with square text wrapping" and is rectangular with a metal frame.

 *Practice*

- Insert any picture into your document and experiment with some of the features in the Picture Tools Format tab. Save the file with the picture and layout you like best.

Clip Art

If you click on Insert > Clip Art, a task pane will open up on the right side of your screen. You can search for a general term and see what clip arts are available online or on your computer. For example, you can search for "Ice cream", find the one you like, click on it or you can right click and select Insert. You have the same formatting options that were available with pictures.

 *Practice*

- Insert any clip art you like into your document. Format it as you wish.

Shapes

This insert feature is easy to understand; however, take a minute to scroll through and see all of the shapes that are available.

 Practice

- Insert at least one shape into your document.

Grouping Objects

To be able to work with objects, shapes, or pictures together, you can group. This can save you time if you want to apply an attribute at the same time.

 Practice

Insert three shapes (without text for now); we will group the three of them.

Hold the Ctrl key down and click on each shape.

Under Drawing tools, under Format tab/Arrange group, click 🔲, then click Group.

Then you can format all three at once.

They can be moved around as a group. If you want to ungroup them to work with them individually, click on the group, then under Drawing tools, under Format tab/Arrange group, click ▦ ,then click Ungroup.

SmartArt

SmartArt can really make your document look more professional. If you click on the icon, you can see all of the choices available. There are even tips to tell you what the choices can best be used for. After selecting SmartArt, two formatting tabs are available to help you select the most effective format.

You can resize the SmartArt.

You can add more choices.

You can change the shape or color.

✔ Practice

- Insert a SmartArt diagram into your document. Enter any text you like and use formatting options to dress it up.

Chart

Charts can be a little confusing if you aren't familiar with how to make a table or spreadsheet. Let's say we want to graph the following information:

Sales	North	$5,000
	South	$3,500
	East	$7,500
	West	$10,000

When you click on insert chart, MS Word will open up a task box so that you can select the type of chart you want. Select the chart that most clearly shows the point you are trying to make (If you need help knowing which chart to use, check the Help or search online.). Then a spreadsheet will open up so that you can type in

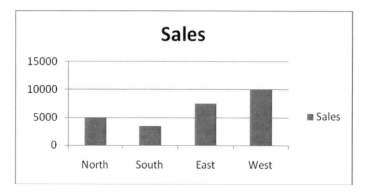

your information. Columns that you aren't using can be deleted by right-clicking on the letter at the top and selecting delete. If your chart is too big, the sizing handles at the corners of the chart can be used to resize it; simply click on them and drag the outline in to where you want it.

 *Practice*

- Insert a small chart into your document; you can select a pie chart, bar chart, or whatever you like.

Hyperlinks

To set up a link to another document, a Web page, or even another location in the current document, you can create a hyperlink. For example, with Insert > Hyperlink, I can enter "My favorite Web site" under Text to Display and type the Web site address of my favorite site and press Enter. This link: <u>My favorite Web</u> site will then take you to my favorite Web site.

 *Practice*

- Insert a hyperlink to your favorite Web site in your document.

Lines

The following are shortcuts for adding lines across the page. Note: you will need to type three of the symbols for it to work.

- Entering *** then pressing Enter will give you a dotted line as shown.

....

- Entering === then pressing Enter will give you a double line as shown.

_____

- Entering ### then pressing Enter will give you a wavy line as shown.

_____

- Entering — — — then pressing Enter will give you a single line as shown.

_____

- Entering ~~~ then pressing Enter will give you a wavy line as shown.

~~~~~~

Headers and Footers

These can be used if you want the same information to appear on each page of your document. Perhaps you want your filename, the date, the page number, or your name to appear on each page. Some of these are already set up for you, so all you have to do is select them—these are called Quick Parts.

When you click on Header (for the top of the page) or Footer (for the bottom of the page), you will first need to select the format of the header. There are some built-in formats or you can prepare a custom header/footer.

If you select one of the built-in formats, the page view will change and a Design tab will open up. From that tab, you can select a Quick Part, change the location of the header, designate if it will be only on certain pages, etc. Notice that the location of the cursor is where the data will show up. For example, if I select a header format with three pieces of data and I click on the center location and then select Page Number, the page number will be in the center at the top of the page.

To close that tab and return to the Normal view, close Header and Footer.

It can be a good idea to have the filename in a footer so that you will be able to find the file if you have a printout, but can't remember what it was named.

✔ Practice

- Insert a footer using one of the built-in formats with the filename (use the Quick Part/Field) on the left and the date on the right.

Text Box, Word Art, Signature Line, Date and Time, Equation

This is a Text Box. You can resize it and select from several formats.

10/29/2009 04:11 PM (date and time)

$$\frac{-b \pm \sqrt{b^2 - 4ac}}{2a}$$ (equation)

✗ _____

(signature line)

These are all features that can save a lot of time if they are items you would use often.

✔ Practice

- Insert examples of each of these five items into your document.

Page Layout Tab

We have done a lot of work on our document about something in our lives. Now let's work on how it will look when we print it out. Notice on the Page Layout tab, you can select a different Theme with different color options (they give you groups of colors to pick from so that it is color coordinated).

You can also:

- Change the margins on the page – Word makes it easy by providing options.

- Change the orientation of the print – portrait or landscape (printing 8½ × 11 or 11 × 8½)

- Control page breaks and hyphenation.

- Line Numbers allows you to number all of the lines in the document. You can try it and then select it again and click None to delete them (or Ctrl z).

These options and more are also accessible by clicking on the arrow next to Page Setup. Notice most options can be applied to the entire document or part of it.

Other options on this tab include:

- Watermarks – these are words that appear in light print across the page behind the text; for example "Confidential", "File Copy", or whatever text you type in.

- Page color – can make your document more attractive on the screen, but remember, if you have a black and white printer, it will still print black and white. If you want a color printout, used colored paper.

- Page borders – are great for flyers, advertisements, etc. They make information stand out.

- Paper size – letter size (standard 8½ by 11), legal size, envelopes, etc.

✔ Practice

- Change your document to Landscape and select margin settings.

- Insert line numbers in the entire document then undo it.

- Add a watermark and border.

Sections and Page Breaks

The Page Layout also allows you to change where a new page starts. If you don't change it, the software will automatically fill a page before going to the next one; setting a manual page break will override that.

If you want a section of your paper to be formatted differently than the rest of the document, you can create a section break. This might be used if you want a different header or footer, or if you need only one page to be landscape.

References Tab

These features are useful for preparing formal reports: footnotes, table of contents, indexing, etc. You can also use footnotes to define a word that users might not comprehend.*

Mailings Tab

Businesses still use mailings for marketing, billings, regular business correspondence, and for many other purposes. If you send mailings to the same people over and over, and there are several of them, the easiest way is to keep a list of their names, addresses, etc., in a word processing file, spreadsheet file, or database file, and then merge that list with the letter, brochure or document you are sending them. This way, you only need to type the letter once. This is called a Mail Merge. MS Word Help has step-by-step instructions for mail merge.

Review Tab

Checking your spelling and grammar should be done even though most programs identify words that are misspelled as you type them. Just remember that software can't catch everything; if ewe are spelling the word write but it is the wrong word, the software might knot catch it.

---

* understand. (notice I changed the footnote from a number to a *)

Other helpful features:

- Thesaurus – if you tend to be using the same words over and over or need more professional language, type the word, select it, right click and pick Synonyms (or select it and click on Thesaurus)

- Translate – you can translate to and from various languages

- Comment – if you want to comment on a document, this will add a comment in the right column. However, it also changes the appearance of the document on the screen. It can be helpful if you are working with a team and have editing suggestions.

- Track changes – this is helpful for working with a team to see what changes have been made in a document

- Compare – this allows you to compare two versions of a document, e.g., someone suggests changes to a document and you want to see the differences from the original

- Protect Document – in case you want to keep others from modifying your document.

- Run a spelling and grammar check on your document and correct any errors.

- Use the thesaurus to change one of the words in your document.

- Add a comment to your paper and notice the way it reformats your paper, and then delete it.

View Tab

Remember the view can be changed quickly by clicking on the buttons in the bottom right corner of the screen, but this tab has several other options. Click on the following to see what they do; they are toggle buttons, so you can click on them again, to switch back.

- Ruler
- Gridlines
- Thumbnails
- Zoom
- Two pages
- New window – this opens a second copy of your file; you can close it
- Viewing side by side allows you to view two documents at the same time, perhaps to compare them or combine them.

Office Button and Quick Access Toolbar

The Office Button has several features, most of them we've used already—New, Open, Print. However, an important one is the Print Preview button (shortcut, Ctrl F2). Get in the habit of always previewing documents before printing them. You can also set Print Preview up on your Quick Access Toolbar; click on the arrow at the top and put checkmarks by the items you want to access quickly.

 Practice

- Use Print Preview to preview your document.

- Print your document.

OpenOffice.org Writer

Let's look at another word processing software package. Now that you understand many features of one software package, it should be easy to learn how to use another one. The icons and buttons might be different, but the features are basically the same.

If you haven't already done so, download OpenOffice.org. Remember it's free. Look at some of the buttons on the toolbar. Many formatting buttons are similar to MS Word— bold, font type, font size, italics, centering, etc.

Many options under File and Insert are also similar:

✓ Practice

- See if you can use OpenOffice.org Writer to create the document you made in MS Word. It isn't necessary to use all of the features, but try to use the common ones.

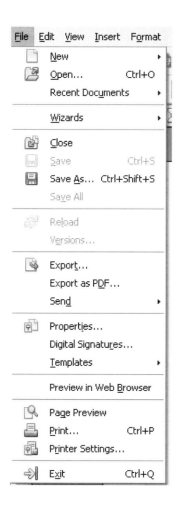

Google Docs

Online software is becoming more popular as people need to collaborate with others. Google docs is free Web-based word processing software that you can use online. When you create your document, it is saved online and you are given a link for it.

Open a browser and go to docs.google.com. You might need to open an account and give them your junk e-mail account.

The options under New are:

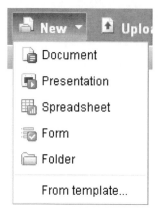

Select New Document. These options should be familiar by now.

Google Docs Menus

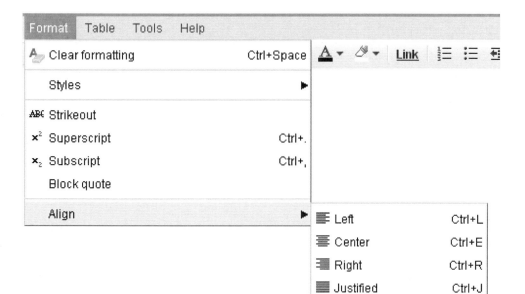

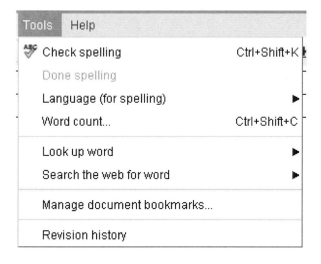

Many of the features in the other menus are similar, too. In fact, the shortcuts (Ctrl z for undo) are often the same, making it easy to transition to a different software package.

The selections under Table aren't available until a Table is inserted. Then, after you insert a table, click on it and you can use any of these features.

So, you can see that the features aren't as numerous as in MS Word, but the main choices are available. Create the same paragraphs you did in MS Word and OpenOffice.org Writer to see how the software compares.

When you complete it, Save it - File > Save, or Ctrl s, or click on the diskette picture.

Notice that you weren't asked to name the file. It has been saved online and given a link.

Click on Share. Here are your options: you can e-mail it to people to collaborate with you or to view it. In the lower part of the screen, you can decide if you would like collaborators to invite others, or invitations to be used by anyone. Uncheck those boxes, enter your e-mail address in the box, and click on invite collaborators.

A screen will open up so that you can write a message. If this were for a work project, for example, you would type something like, "Chris, this is a draft of the letter we discussed. Please review it and make any changes you think should be made. Thanks."

Type a little message in the box so you can see what it will look like. For example, you can type "from me" or whatever you like.

For this practice, don't check the box for pasting the document into the e-mail message.

Press Send.

Close out the screen it returns to (X), save and close the document, and check your e-mail. Clicking on the link should open up your document.

Word Processing Projects

1. Create a letter using a template in Open Office.org Writer. To download a letter template, Open OpenOffice.org Writer > File > New > Templates and Documents > Get more templates online > Search for letter. Select any of the formal letter templates you would like to download. Choose one of the following topics for your letter:

   a. Topics

      i. Letter to your favorite restaurant asking if you can rent a room for a party

      ii. Letter to a movie producer suggesting a movie idea

      iii. Letter to a character in a TV show from another character in the same show

      iv. Letter to your magic genie about your dream job

      v. Letter to a friend about your favorite charity and why they should help with the next fundraiser

   b. Your letter should have:

      i. At least three paragraphs

      ii. All of the parts of a letter—date, address of recipient, your address, salutation, closing, etc. (it can all be made up)

      iii. Complete sentences, no misspellings, no grammatical errors

      iv. Try to use the "you-viewpoint," focusing on the reader's point of view. (This one is not all about you.)

2. MS Word – Working with one or two other people, write a newsletter about college life. Your newsletter should be one-page long and have:

   a. Two columns

   b. Bullets

   c. A clip art or picture

   d. A table with at least two columns and three rows

   e. At least one dropped cap (use Help if you don't know how to do this)

   f. A hyperlink

   g. Any other features that you think will make it a great newsletter

3. Google docs – Working with one or two other people, evaluate two or three Web sites. Collaboratively develop a document critiquing the sites that has:

   i. Benefits and disadvantages of the sites (which loads quickly, which is your favorite, etc.)

   ii. Any of the features you want to use in Google docs

   iii. The review should be at least 200 words long.

   iv. Share the file with your instructor, but make sure it has the name of the creators. (Make sure you share it, insert your instructor's e-mail address, and select the instructor as a collaborator.

4. This Comfort Zone Project* requires some original research.

    a. Goal of project: to enhance your skills for entering a new or uncomfortable setting and navigating successfully within it and using word processing software

    b. Length: the paper should be at least one full page, single spaced

    c. Charge: Pick a group that differs from you in ethnicity, religion, or sexual orientation and which you are unfamiliar and/or uncomfortable with. Then go to a setting where you will find this group and report on your experiences and reactions. It could be an area of town, cultural center, a religious setting, or a restaurant/bar frequented by the group.

    d. In your paper, discuss the following:

        i. Why did you pick the setting? How does visiting there extend your comfort zone?

        ii. What did you see? What was the demographic makeup of the setting? What patterns of behavior and interaction did you observe?

        iii. How did you feel and behave?

        iv. What did you learn? What strategies have you developed for navigating within this setting in the future? What tips can you offer concerning how to connect with people in this setting?

    e. Type the paper in MS Word using the following features and any others that are appropriate:

        i. SmartArt

        ii. WordArt

        iii. Picture or Clip Art

        iv. At least two different fonts and font sizes

        v. Centering

        vi. A footnote explaining something in the paper or referencing something

        vii. Single spacing, justified

---

* Special thanks to Dr. Dale Rude, Associate Professor at the University of Houston, for this project idea.

chapter 5

THE GLOBAL BUSINESS ENVIRONMENT

STUDENT LEARNING OUTCOMES

After successfully completing this chapter, students will be able to:

1. Demonstrate a functional understanding of the nature and importance of enterprise resource planning systems.

2. Explain the steps in a business process and give examples of input and output for major functional areas in a business.

Globalization and Technology

The world has become a much smaller place. Students communicate in real time with students in other countries or even take classes from a school in another country; sales of products happen across countries continuously; people play online games with gamers in different countries; people with similar interests e-mail, text, chat, or blog with like-minded people anywhere in the world; and production of products happens anywhere in the world. This means that the companies producing these products, games, websites, and services need to operate globally, not locally. This means adapting to time changes, languages, currency differences, technology, infrastructures, cultures, and environments. Technology is the only way to coordinate global transactions efficiently.

Communication and up-to-date information are crucial. If we own a company that sells toothbrushes manufactured in Japan, we can't order 100 billion toothbrushes in January for the entire year. We need to order based on demand—we might sell more than 100 billion in a year, or we may sell less. Or in February, scientists may develop a way for people to keep their teeth clean without toothbrushes, and we end up with 100 billion toothbrushes we can't sell. Businesses, especially global ones, rely on technology to give them accurate, real-time information to make decisions.

Issues to Consider

When designing for a global economy, there are many factors to consider. For example, if we are designing a search engine, we need to write it in as many languages as we can. We should also include translation capabilities so users can translate pages from other languages. It is difficult to prevent all misunderstandings, and often websites don't translate accurately. There are many examples of miscommunication. For example, a detour sign in Japan translates to "Stop: Drive Sideways".

Also, wherever our servers are housed, they need to be reliable, and we need to be able to communicate with the employees at that location. Another important factor to consider is the culture of other countries. Is directness a good quality? Is it polite to address individuals by their first name? What words are considered impolite, rude, or X-rated?

Business Processes

In business terms, everything is a process broken down into **Input > Processing > Output**. For example, we **input** your hourly rate, social security number, hours worked this week (and some more data); **process** the data (multiply hourly rate by hours worked, deduct taxes, etc.); and the **output** is your paycheck, woohoo! Notice that this business process requires data from more than one department—human resources provides data such as hiring date and social security number, your supervisor provides the number of hours you worked that week, and the payroll department processes the data and produces the payment either in the form of a check or as a direct deposit to your bank account.

One of the core business processes of a company is the fulfillment process, producing goods or services and getting them to the customers. To explain processes better, we will focus on this process. However, instead of toothbrushes, let's say we manufacture ice cream. We sell to stores that sell directly to the customer. So, our fulfillment process is:

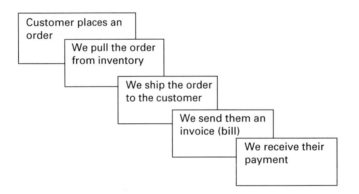

Notice we aren't concerned with ordering the raw materials (chocolate, milk, vanilla, etc.) for the ice cream and we aren't concerned with making the ice cream. Obtaining the raw materials for the ice cream happens during the **procurement process** and making the ice cream happens during the **production process**. We are going to focus on the **fulfillment process**—getting our ice cream to the stores (customers) to sell.

Notice, also, that we left out many steps, such as checking to make sure the inventory is in stock at a nearby warehouse, giving customers a quantity discount, perhaps getting some of the ice cream back if it's not what they wanted, etc. We are just looking at the basic steps for now to understand the process.

Business Activities

Each of the departments or functional areas of an organization performs activities that make up the business processes. For example, Human Resources (HR) might interview employees, perform background checks, and hire employees. Once the employee is hired, HR inputs the data (name, birth date, social security number, address, department, position, etc.) into the system. If the president of the company wants a list of all employees, the data is **processed** and a report (**output**) is generated.

The key here is that everything should be integrated. Each of the departments in a business has data and they all need data from each other. Here are a few examples.

Department or Functional Area	What They Do	Data They Have	Data They May Need From Other Areas
Accounting and Finance	Handles all of the financial aspects that must be integrated within the entire organization	• Interest made on investments • Customer credit data information	• Salary figures • Projected cost of advertising promotions
Human Resources	Handles all personnel information, including background checks, training, etc.	• Salary figures • Employee contact information	• Job openings to be filled • Raises for employees
Marketing and Sales	Handles sales, advertising, deliveries, works with customers	• Projected cost of advertising promotions • Orders from customers	• Budget available for advertising • When production of new items will occur
Supply Chain Management	Produces the product, ordering raw materials, etc.	• Raw materials needed for production • Inventory levels	• Which products are going to be advertised • Pay rates of employees

Once you have taken more business classes, you will know more about what data the various departments have and what they need from other departments.

Enterprise Resource Planning (ERP) Systems

When you register for school, you are probably using an ERP system.

- You are in the system as a client/customer of the school with data such as your address, phone number, and e-mail address;

- you are in the system as a potential library user with data such as your ability to access the online library and to check out materials;

- you are in the system as a potential health center user with data such as your allergies, last flu shot, and visits to the center;

- you might be in the system as an employee if you work on campus with data such as your pay rate, which department you work in, social security number, and your skills;

- and, of course, you are in the system as a student with data such as your major, classes taken, GPA, grades, etc.

You can imagine how much easier it is to have one huge database for all of the departments instead of individual ones. That way, once your student ID number and basic data are entered in, they would be available to everyone in the system so that they don't have to enter it themselves. Not only would the people at the school (the employees of the company) be able to use the system, it would also give you (the customer) the ability to register online and check your grades. This huge database, made up of many related tables, is an ERP system.

Many companies use ERP systems, no matter what their product is: fast food restaurants, clothing stores, banks, hospitals, petroleum plants, shoe manufacturers, etc. The ERP software will be designed or customized for that specific industry and business.

A Common Database

Whether you work in accounting, sales, marketing, human resources (personnel) or manufacturing, your department will need information from the system. So, you can see that it will be useful for all business majors to understand a little about how ERP programs work.

There are several advantages to using ERP systems. Primarily, they improve data accuracy and limit redundancy. If your last name is Stegosaurus, it is probably often misspelled. If one person enters your data into the computer and others in the company are able to access it, you eliminate the possibility that your name is entered five different times with five different spellings, e.g., Stagosaurus, Stegesaurus, Stegasaurus.

Even if your name is Joe Smith, which most people probably won't misspell, it can save a lot of time if only one person has to enter it instead of five. Mistakes in keying information happen often, even on easy words.

Another advantage is that the business is integrated with ERP systems. All departments work together and rely on each other, so ERP systems allow users to obtain the data they need quickly without contacting the other department every time they need it. If we work in sales and receive an order for 500 cases of ice cream, we can check the inventory level online without having to call over to the warehouse to see if we have 500 cases. This is important at all levels of the organization. The president can quickly obtain reports needed for decision making without having to send a memo and wait for the information.

Many steps can be automated. The system can be designed and programmed to automatically order more chocolate chips when supply reaches a certain level. It can be programmed to determine which supplier meets our criteria (i.e., high quality chocolate, proximity to the plant, availability) and handle the transaction without human intervention.

Features

There are several things that organizations look for in ERP systems. One of the most important features is scalability. The system needs to be able to handle a large number of users. Client server architecture makes this easy and provides flexibility. The database server that houses the program might be housed in El Paso, Texas. From that database server, we can have many application servers in various locations and countries. Each of those application servers can have many users. You've probably seen this design in a computer lab. You might be connected to a server at a different location where you can store information (files) and you can also be networked to share devices such as printers.

ERP systems continue to evolve and become more user friendly, now using web-based applications.

In IT, a distinction is made between data (raw facts) and information (processed data that has meaning). The following data: Joe, Henry, Sally, Sue, 54, 48, 69, and 47 don't mean anything until we process it into a table such as the following:

Employee First Name	Employee Hourly Rate
Sally	69
Joe	54
Henry	48
Sue	47

[You probably thought those were their ages.]

It's also helpful to know the difference between transaction data and master data. Transaction data describes an event and is relatively temporary, e.g., data about a sale that was made. Master data, also called reference data, is relatively permanent data that is often shared across an organization. The standard example is customer data—the name, address, and type of customer won't change often, but they will be used by various functional areas of the company. Master Data Management is becoming more and more important. We don't want to lose a valued customer because we didn't update their new address in our system. Likewise, we don't want to keep offering discounts to a customer who doesn't pay their bills.

SAP

In 1972, five former IBM employees began a company called Systems, Analysis, and Program Development (SAP) in Germany. Notice that SAP is pronounced S-A-P (like L-O-L), not sap. SAP is now one of the world's largest ERP vendors. It is in more than 75,000 locations, in more than 100 countries, and used by more than 10 million people each day. SAP modules include SD (Sales and Distribution), MM (Materials Management), HR (Human Resources), and PP (Production Planning).

 Projects

Search online for funny translations. What are five of the funniest or strangest translations you discovered? (Not X-rated, please.)

1. _____

List two ERP systems besides SAP.

2. _____

List four companies that don't use SAP software. What ERP systems do they use?

3. _____

Assume we work at a local fast food restaurant. We sell burgers, fries, shakes, etc. List three different jobs in the company and three pieces of data they would each provide and three pieces of data they would need from someone else. Be specific, e.g., the number of pounds of potatoes to cook in the month of January.

4. _____

Describe how the SD process would work for our fast food business. What are the steps?

5. _____

Research SAP. What are some of the different industries and companies that use SAP (e.g., clothing manufacturing, Under Armour)? List at least five.

6. _____

What are two additional interesting facts that you discovered about SAP?

7. _____

SPREADSHEETS

STUDENT LEARNING OUTCOMES

After successfully completing this chapter, students will be able to:

1. Demonstrate use of advanced spreadsheet features such as charts, graphs, absolute reference formulas, and IF formulas.

2. Demonstrate proficiency in developing basic business spreadsheets such as revenue and expense statements, budgets, cash flow analyses, and perform calculations for various accounting and financial ratios.

3. Develop spreadsheets which link multiple documents, automatically update information from an Internet source, perform regression, and utilize data analysis tools.

Spreadsheets are used for files that have numbers and calculations and for databases (collections of data).

Openoffice.org Calc

Excel:

The real advantage in using spreadsheets is that since formulas are used instead of simply typing in numbers, if any figure changes, the entire spreadsheet is re-calculated instantly.

Most spreadsheet software is similar; once you learn one package, you can easily transition to a different one. (Some examples will be shown in OpenOffice and MS Excel.) Also, several spreadsheet features are the same as in the word processing software, so the first part is a review.

File New or Office Button New – to open a blank page

File Open or Office Button Open – to open an existing file

File Save or Office Button Save – to save a file the first time

File Save As or Office Button Save As – to save the file under a different name and/or under a different file type (e.g., to save on OpenOffice Calc file as an MS Excel file)

Ctrl C – copy

Ctrl V – paste

Ctrl X – cut

Ctrl Z – undo

 *Practice*

1. Open a new spreadsheet and save it on your flash drive as Excel practice 1.

Cells – Spreadsheets are all about numbers. To make it easier to work with individual numbers, everything is entered in boxes called cells. Words are also entered into cells, either individually or in groups depending on the purpose. For example, the words in a title or heading would all be entered in one cell. Categories like company A, company B, January, and February would each be entered in a separate cell. Cell locations are identified by the column letter and row number. For example, "Thing 2" is in cell B2.

	A	B	C	D	E	F	G
1	North	Thing 1	1	1	0		
2	North	Thing 2	1	2	5		
3	North	Thing 3	1	3	10		
4	North	Thing 4	1	4	15		
5	North	Thing 5	1	5	20		
6	North	Thing 6	1	6	25		
7	North	Thing 7	1	7	30		
8	North	Thing 8	1	8	35		
9	North	Thing 9	1	9	40		
10	North	Thing 10	1	10	45		

to move – select the outside border and drag the cell

to copy/fill – use the bottom right black square

Spreadsheet practice 1.ods - OpenOffice.org Calc

File   Edit   View   Insert   Format   Tools   Data   Window   Help

Arial   10   B   I   U

D12

Sheet1 / Sheet2 / Sheet3

Sheet 1 / 3   Default   STD   *   Sum=0

Moving in Spreadsheets

You can move easily to any cell in a spreadsheet—empty or not—using the arrow keys or the scroll bars at the right and bottom of the screen. Also, since spreadsheets are huge—hundreds of rows and columns—you can jump around quickly using:

- Ctrl Home to get to A1
- Home to get to the far left of a row
- Page Up
- Page Down
- Ctrl → to get to the last column on the right
- Ctrl ↓ to get to the last row

Also, if you enter a cell location in the box that says L2 in the picture and press enter, you can jump to that cell.

Also, notice that this is just one worksheet; at the bottom of the screen, you can select Sheet 2 and you will open up another worksheet. And, even though there are only three shown, you can create more. A **workbook** is a file containing related worksheets.

Selecting Items in Spreadsheets

<u>To select a cell</u> – click in the center of the cell. To select several cells at one time, drag across, holding the left mouse button down.

<u>To move a cell</u> –
in MS Excel – click on the outside border of the cell.
in OpenOffice – use cut and paste.

✔ Practice

1. How many columns are there on one worksheet in Excel? _____

2. How many rows are there on one worksheet in Excel? _____

3. What is the maximum number of sheets you can have in one Excel workbook? (You may have to "search" or get "help" for this one.) _____

<u>To copy/fill</u> – usually to copy a cell, you will click on the bottom right corner of the cell (on the little black square) and drag the cursor down or across. Sometimes, the software will fill in data. For example,

- If you enter January, and copy/fill to adjacent cells, both OpenOffice and Excel will fill in February, March, etc.
- If you enter 1 and copy/fill to adjacent cells, OpenOffice will fill in 2, 3, etc. Excel will copy the 1.
- If you enter 1 and then a 2, in the next cell, select both of these, and fill down, excel will continue counting.

- If you enter a 5 and then a 10, select both of these and fill down, the software will continue the series (5, 10, 15, 20, 25…).

- If you enter company 1 or thing 1 (or anything then a 1) and copy down, the software will continue counting (company 1, company 2, company 3…).

 Practice

1. Enter the data in the example into your saved spreadsheet and save it again.

Freezing Columns and Rows

We will be working with little spreadsheets as we learn the software, so most likely all of your data will fit on the screen. But, in the real world, spreadsheets may be huge—hundreds of lines long. Scrolling through that can be confusing, especially if you need to see data at the top of the spreadsheet and at the bottom at the same time.

You can freeze columns or rows by grabbing and dragging the freeze bars down or over to where you want them.

This creates a dividing line and you can work or scroll in whichever window you like. To return to the regular view, simply double-click on the dividing line.

	A	B	C	D	
1	North	South	East	West	
2	1				
3	2				
4	3				
5	4				
6	5				
7	6				
8	7				
52	51				
53	52				
54	53				
55	54				
56	55				
57	56				
58	57				

You can also freeze panes by using the Window Group under the View tab in Excel.

Messages

The following messages may appear after you have entered data or a formula in a cell if there is something you need to correct:

######	Your column isn't wide enough—widen it
#DIV/0	You are attempting to divide by 0
#N/A	Value isn't available—the formula needed a number for calculation
#Name?	The text isn't recognized
#Ref?	Invalid cell reference

You might also see a tiny triangle/smart tag that will pull up more information in Excel. For example, you can set a smart tag to link to financial symbols. Clicking on the smart tag next to MSFT gives you the options shown since MSFT is a stock symbol.

Formatting

Effective formatting makes the spreadsheet look better and makes it easier to understand the information. Many formatting features are the same in spreadsheets as in word processing, and many of them are in the same place on the Home tab. To format, you select the cell and then select the formatting feature. Or you can format the cell before entering data in it.

Locate the icons for the following:

- Font type, size
- Bold (or ctrl b), italics (or ctrl i), underlining (or ctrl u)
- Centering, left alignment, right alignment
- Borders (around the cell, right, left, top, bottom, double bottom border)

✔ Practice

1. Open the spreadsheet you created.
2. Practice using the following features on several cells to become familiar with them. Remember you can select several cells at the same time to apply the same formatting feature to them.
   - Change the font size.
   - Use italics.
   - Use borders around some cells trying different variations—only bottom border, top and bottom, left and right, etc.
   - Use a different color of text.
   - Change the font type.
   - Use bold.
   - Rotate text.
   - Underline.
   - Use a different color background.

To change the format of the entire spreadsheet, you can press ctrl and "a" to select everything or click on the cell to the left of column A and above row 1 to select everything.

	A	B	C	D	E	F	G	
1		January	February	March	April	May	June	
2	State 1	1	0	1	14	100	50	
3	State 2	1	5	2	35	200	50	
4	State 3	1	10	3	81	300	50	
5	State 4	1	15	4	62	400	50	
6	State 5	1	20	5	15	500	50	
7	State 6	1	25	6	65	600	50	
8								
9	click on the square to select All							
10								

There are many more features that you can access by selecting the cell, right clicking, and selecting Format Cells or by opening a dialog box (clicking on the small arrow on the bottom row of the Font group on Excel).

✔ Practice

1. Open a new spreadsheet and create the spreadsheet with the months and states. Remember to use the fill feature to save time, i.e., type January and use fill to enter the other months.

2. Add as many formatting features as you can to make it look more attractive.

3. Use Select All to change a formatting feature on the entire spreadsheet.

Inserting Pictures, Clip Art, Shapes, and SmartArt

The options for inserting the items listed above are the same as in MS Word. Please refer to that chapter if you need an explanation of any of those items.

Formatting Numbers

There are several standard choices on the Home tab:

Currency, Percentages, standard number formatting, increase or decrease digits to the right of the decimal, indent in a cell or decrease indent in a cell, etc.

More choices can be found by right clicking on any of those icons in OpenOffice Calc or by opening the Number dialog box in Excel (small arrow to the right of Number on the Home tab).

✔ Practice

1. Click on one cell with numbers in it and change it to currency.

2. Click on one cell and change it to currency with no decimals.

3. Format some cells for percentage.

4. Use the indention feature for several cells.

The Paintbrush

You can save a great deal of time with the paintbrush both in Calc and Excel. If you have a cell or a range of cells formatted the way you want them and want to copy the format ONLY (not the data, words, numbers), select the formatted cells, click on the paintbrush, and click on the cells you want formatted the same way.

Paste Options

There are several options for pasting data you have copied or moved, e.g., you may want to paste just the contents of the cell without the format, or just the values.

Merge Cells

Another formatting feature that can improve the appearance of your spreadsheet is the merge feature. The following spreadsheet looks fine, but it would look so much better if the title "Sales" were centered across all four columns.

	A	B	C	D
1	**Sales**			
2		Price	Quantity	Extension
3	Guitar	$750.00	15	$11,250.00
4	Drum	$600.00	21	$12,600.00
5	Microphone	$250.00	9	$2,250.00
6	Music	$20.00	53	$1,060.00
7	Drumsticks	$15.00	26	$390.00
8				

To do this, select cells A1 through D1 with the mouse. Then click on:

Calc Format > Merge Cells then click on ☰ to center

Excel Click on ⊞ ▾ (home tab, alignment group, bottom row, far right)

Working with Columns

To make changes to a column, select the letter at the top of that column. To make changes to a row, select the number of the row. Right clicking on the letter or number will pull up more options:

A quicker way to change the column width is to click on the line between the two letters (or numbers on the row) and slide it over to increase or decrease the column width. Also, if you double-click on the line between the columns, the width will automatically be set to the width of the longest item in the column.

	A	B	C	
1				
2				
3				
4				
5				
6	Click here to change the column width			
7	Double-click to autoset the width			
8				

You can also select more than one column by clicking on the first one, holding the left mouse button, and dragging across to the others.

✔ Practice

1. With the spreadsheet you just worked on, insert two columns.

2. Insert two rows.

3. Change the columns to 10.00 width.

4. Change the row heights.

5. Use the software to change a few of the columns to the width they need to be to fit the data in those columns.

More Formatting

You can easily use color and fonts to make your spreadsheets more attractive. Excel also has several styles already created for you to select from.

✔ Practice

Type this easy spreadsheet:

	A	B	C	D	
1		January	February	March	
2	Sugar	6	5	7	
3	Chocolate chip	5	4	7	
4	Peanut butter	5	3	4	
5					
6					

In OpenOffice.org Calc, there are a few preset styles and formats that you can access by selecting Format > Styles and Formatting.

To try it in OpenOffice.org Calc, select January, February, and March > Format > Styles and Formatting (or F11) > double-click on one of the Heading formats.

Excel also has preset cell formats—get to them by clicking on Cell Styles:

To use the preset Table formats in Excel, click on Format as Table:

A few interesting things happen if you select Format as Table in Excel. First, Excel will ask you where your data is for the table. Select all of the cells including the top and side headings. Notice that you can check the box indicating that you have headings.

The appearance of your table will change because Excel added some other shortcuts. These make it easier to sort a column, e.g., from smallest to largest.

✔ Practice

1. Create the cookie table in Excel.

2. Format the cookie spreadsheet as a table.

3. Sort by a few of the columns so that you can see how it works.

Obviously there are more features in the table format. The filters feature makes it easy to narrow down a huge database. For example, if we are only interested in the data for sugar cookies, you can select Number Filters > equals > enter "Sugar". The filter will list the data for Sugar cookies.

Conditional Formatting

Conditional formatting will change the formatting of cells only if they meet the condition you specify. For example, perhaps the boss wants the cookies that are selling more than five cases a month to stand out in the table.

To use conditional formatting:

- Select all of the cells with numbers in them (except the Total numbers).

- In OpenOffice.org Calc go to Format > Conditional Formatting > select Greater Than and in the blank box to the right, enter 5 > for cell style, select Result > click OK.

- In Excel, click on Conditional Formatting > Highlight Cell Rules > great than > enter 5 > click on the arrow next to "light red fill" to see the other preset options and select one > click OK.

The following picture uses conditional formatting that underlines and places the numbers in bold font if they meet the criteria (greater than 5). Excel offers more options for conditional formatting.

	A	B	C	D	E
1		January	February	March	
2	Sugar	6	5	7	
3	Chocolate chip	5	4	7	
4	Peanut butter	5	3	4	
5	Totals	16	12	18	
6					

Insert and Page Layout Tabs

Take a minute to look at the Insert and the Page Layout tabs in Excel. You should be familiar with the following features from those tabs:

Insert Tab:	Page Layout Tab:
Picture	Margins
Clip Art	Orientation
Shapes	Size
SmartArt	Breaks
Text Box	
Header and Footer	
WordArt	
Signature Line	
Symbol	
Hyperlink	

Charts

Although we are able to insert charts in word processing programs, they are often better in spreadsheet programs since we are dealing with numbers. One of the most important things when charting data is to pick the right graph; this is the one that tells your audience what you want them to know. Excel helps users select the right chart by identifying times when a certain chart should be used. For example, place your cursor over the Line Chart. The hint "Line charts are used to display trends over time" displays. This is a good chart to show how sales over the past five years have grown (or not).

✔ Practice

Before trying this for practice, make sure you don't have any blank rows or columns in your cookie spreadsheet. If you do, delete them by right clicking on the column letter or row number and selecting delete.

The easiest way to insert a chart is to select the data you want graphed ahead of time. Using your cookie spreadsheet, select all of the data except the Total row; make sure you include the kinds of cookies and the months.

Select data > Click on column > select the specific type you want > there is your chart!

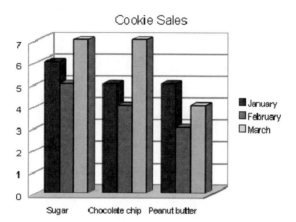

And notice that three more tabs opened up as long as the table is selected: Design, Layout, and Format. Creating a simple chart is so easy, anyone can do it. Learn to design charts that stand out from the beginners by using the design features that are available. You can even create a combination chart, e.g., one with a line chart and bar chart in the same chart.

1. The Design tab allows you do use different chart styles, switch the rows and columns if you need to, quickly select a chart layout that might move the legend and give you a template for a chart title.

2. The Layout tab has several important features: title, legend, data labels, axes, and gridlines.

3. The Format tab allows users to make the charts more attractive or to make one piece of data stand out. For example you can change the shape style on one piece of the chart (e.g., select one bar and then apply the style) or the entire chart.

Apply some of the features to your cookie chart—add a title, change the color or style of some parts of your chart.

Viewing Options in Excel

Similar to Word, you can view your spreadsheet in Normal View, Page Layout View, and Page Break View. The easiest way to change views is to use the icons in the bottom right corner.

Notice that the zoom bar is there also.

Graphing Non-Adjacent Data

That graph was pretty easy, but maybe we want to graph the totals for the months, but not the monthly data. It's still easier to select everything you want graphed at the beginning. Select the months, hold down the Ctrl key, and select the totals as shown (not the Total heading).

Now follow the same steps – Insert > select chart type.

Formulas, Equations, Math!

Making a nice-looking table is good, but the best part of spreadsheet programs is their ability to do math, statistics, and lots of equations quickly and easily. To understand the real beauty of the program, we need a bigger spreadsheet, but let's start out with a small one. Delete a couple of lines from your cookie spreadsheet:

We want to add the two numbers for January and place the answer in B4. Here are a few ways to do this:

Click on B4 > enter = 6+5 > press Enter

or

Click on B4 > type = B2+B3 > press Enter

or

Click on B4 > type = > click on B2 > type + > click on B3 > press Enter

The first way isn't good because if the numbers change, you have to type in the formula again. The second way is ok, but most people type pretty slowly. The third way is good because you can select the cells. The fourth method (shown below) is the best:

OpenOffice.org Calc

Click on B4 > click on Σ > notice that Calc puts a box around the two numbers that it thinks you want to add (and it's right!); if it is right, press Enter

Excel

Click on B4 > click on Σ > notice that Excel puts dashed lines around the two numbers that it thinks you want to add (and it's right!); if it is right, press Enter or click on Σ again.

This is quick and easy, but what if those weren't the numbers we wanted to add. Let's say we want to put the answer in cell A4 as shown:

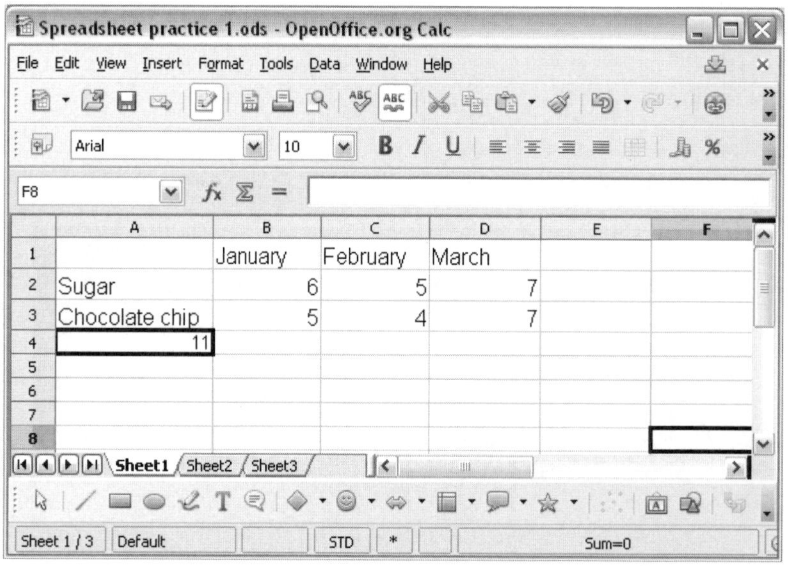

In Calc

Click on A4 > then click on Σ > Calc has no idea what you want to add since the cells above aren't numbers; select cells B2 and B3 with the mouse > press Enter

In Excel

Click on A4 > then click on Σ > Excel has no idea what you want to add either since the cells above aren't numbers; select cells B2 and B3 with the mouse > press Enter

Ok, great, but other things can throw the formula off, like if there is an empty cell somewhere in the range you want to add. The software, using Sum, will stop if it encounters a blank cell. In the example, Calc will only add B6 since the cell above is empty. To correct it, simply use the mouse to select the entire range from B2 to B6.

Spreadsheet practice 1.ods - OpenOffice.org Calc

File Edit View Insert Format Tools Data Window Help

Arial   12   B I U

SUM   =SUM(B6)

	A	B	C	D	E	F
1		January				
2	Sugar	6				
3	Chocolate chip	5				
4	Peanut Butter	8				
5	Frosted					
6	Oatmeal	3				
7		=SUM(B6)				
8						
9						

Sheet1 Sheet2 Sheet3

Sheet 1 / 3   Default   INSRT   STD   *   Sum=0

✔ Practice

1. Complete the cookie spreadsheet as shown (use data fill when you can to save time).

Spreadsheet practice 1.ods - OpenOffice.org Calc

File Edit View Insert Format Tools Data Window Help

Arial   10   B I U

F10

	A	B	C	D	E	F
1		January	February	March		
2	Sugar	6	4			
3	Chocolate chip	5	6	6		
4	Peanut Butter	8	8	2		
5	Frosted		4	4		
6	Oatmeal	3	1	1		
7	Totals	22	23	13		
8						
9						

Sheet1 Sheet2 Sheet3

Sheet 1 / 3   Default   STD   *   Sum=0

2. Determine the three totals.

When you click on your total cells, you can see the formula = SUM(B2:B6). That's another way you can enter the formula if you like typing.

Viewing the Formulas

If you click on a cell with a formula in it, you can view the formula. Also, if you want to see the entire spreadsheet in Formula View, you can:

- Formulas > Show Formulas
- Or hold down the Ctrl key and press the `key (the key to the left of the 1)

These are toggle buttons; you can select them again to go back to the Normal View.

Maximum, Minimum, Average

Addition is not the only operation that you might use on a column or row of numbers. Finding the highest number in a range (maximum), the lowest number (minimum), and the average can also be done using the same method.

<u>Calc</u>

In Calc, you'll use the f_x (function) key.

Maximum in Calc:

Click on B7 > click on f_x > you can use either the All Category or the Statistical Category > Select Max >

click Next > notice Calc needs you to enter the range for
select the range with your mouse > click OK

Minimum in Calc:

Click on B8 > click on f_x > you can use either the All Category or the Statistical Category > Select Min >

click Next > notice Calc needs you to enter the range for [number 1 f_x B2:B6] select the range with your mouse > click OK

**Make sure you don't include the maximum in your range for minimum. You will get incorrect answers if you don't specify the range accurately.

Average in Calc:

Click on B9 > click on f_x > you can use either the All Category or the Statistical Category > Select Average

> click Next > notice Calc needs you to enter the range for [number 1 f_x B2:B6] select the range with your mouse > click OK

**Make sure you don't include the maximum or minimum cells in your range for the average.

Excel

Excel also has a [f_x] key, but there is an even easier way to perform the three operations we are learning. Notice the little arrow next to the Sum button. If you click on the arrow, you'll see that Average, Max, and Min are there so we can perform these functions the same way we use the Sum button.

Maximum in Excel:

Click on B7 > then click on the arrow next to Sum [Σ] > Select Max > Excel will put a box around the range it thinks is correct > if it is correct > press Enter; if the range is not correct, select the range with your mouse then > press Enter

Minimum in Excel:

Click on B8 > then click on the arrow next to Sum [Σ] > Select Min > Excel will put a box around the range it thinks is correct > if it is correct > press Enter; if the range is not correct, select the range with your mouse then > press Enter

Average in Excel:

Click on B9 > then click on the arrow next to Sum [Σ] > Select Avg > Excel will put a box around the range it thinks is correct > if it is correct > press Enter; if the range is not correct, select the range with your mouse then > press Enter

**Make sure you don't include the maximum or minimum cells in your range for the average.

Other Formulas with Ranges

This method will work with any formulas that have ranges. Notice that another option is to Count the number of items in a range using the Count function. Here are three examples:

1	A	1
2	B	2
3	B	3
4	B	4
5	A	5
6	A	6
7	C	7
8	B	8
9	A	9
10	B	10
=COUNT(F6:F15)	=COUNTIF(H6:H15,"B")	=COUNTIF(J6:J15,5)

The first formula will count the number of items in the range – the answer will be 10 because there are ten numbers.

The second formula will count the number of B's in the range. Notice that you have to use quotations around "B" in the formula. You will use quotations any time a formula uses letters or words. The answer will be 5 because there are five Bs in the range.

The third formula will count the number of 5's in the range – the answer will be 1 because there is one five.

We can also determine the Median or Mode for a range of numbers. You should be able to figure that out.

Subtract, Multiply, Divide

There are many other formulas, but first let's look at more easy ones. For some crazy reason, assume that we are asked to subtract the number of chocolate chip boxes from the number of sugar boxes.

	A	B	C	D	E
1		January	February	March	
2	Sugar	6	6	6	
3	Chocolate chip	5	2	6	
4	Subtract				
5	Multiply				
6	Divide				
7					

Remember—don't type in the answer or enter = 6+5. The numbers will probably change and then we would have to enter the formula again. We want the software to do that for us.

Subtraction

Click on B4 > type = B2 − B3 > press Enter

or

Click on B4 > type = > click on B2 > type − > click on B3 > press Enter

<u>Multiplication</u>

Click on B5 > type = B2 * B3 > press Enter

or

Click on B5 > type = > click on B2 > type * > click on B3 > press Enter

<u>Division</u>

Click on B6 > type = B2/B3 > press Enter

or

Click on B6 > type = > click on B2 > type / > click on B3 > press Enter

✔ Practice

Complete the spreadsheet as shown (using formulas). Don't complete February or March yet.

	A	B January	C February	D March
1		January	February	March
2	Sugar	6	6	6
3	Chocolate chip	5	2	6
4	Subtract	1		
5	Multiply	30		
6	Divide	1.2		
7				

Filling in Formulas

So far, the software may not be saving us too much time, but it can save a lot of time on big spreadsheets, and one of the ways it does this is by allowing us to copy formulas. The fill handle (little black square in the lower right corner of a cell) allows users to copy formulas.

	A	B January	C February	D March
1		January	February	March
2	Sugar	6	6	6
3	Chocolate chip	5	2	6
4	Subtract	1		
5	Multiply	30		
6	Divide	1.2		
7				
8				

Click on the black square in the lower right corner of B4 and, using the mouse, drag over two cells to the right. It should fill in both February and March subtractions. Do the same thing to copy the multiplication and division formulas over to February and March.

Order of Calculations

If you have a cell with a longer equation such as both multiplication and addition, it's important to know which calculations will be done first.

In the following example, to calculate a 10% bonus of the net pay for each employee, D1 should subtract the taxes from salaries (B2 − C2) and then multiply the result by 10%.

If we were to enter this as we've been doing, the formula would be = B2−C2*.10. However, if you try that, the answer for Will is $98,684.60. Does it seem logical that a 10% bonus for an employee making $99,000 is more than $98,000? No!

	A	B	C	D
1		Salaries	Taxes	10% bonus
2	Will	$99,000.00	$3,154.00	
3	Carlton	$98,000.00	$2,415.00	
4	Hilary	$95,487.00	$2,654.00	
5	Ashley	$100,000.00	$9,542.00	
6				

The problem is that spreadsheets process certain functions first—multiplication is processed before addition. To correct our formula, we would simply have to use ( ) around the part of the equation that we want the spreadsheet to perform first.

= (B2 − C2)*.10

Multiplication and division are performed before addition and subtraction. If both multiplication and division are in the same formula, spreadsheets will perform them from left to right. For example, in the following equation = D4/E4*F4, first D4 will be divided by E4, and that answer will be multiplied by F4.

Relative Reference: Location, Location, Location

The reason you can copy formulas like that is because spreadsheets use relative references. What this means is that the formula is relative to the location of the cell the formula is in. For example:

This formula = A1 + B2 entered in C1 means to add the two cells to the left.

It doesn't mean add cell A1 to cell B2; it means add the two cells to the left.

If A1 = 1 and B1 = 1, it still doesn't mean 1 + 1; it means add the two cells to the left.

So, as long as you want to add the two cells to the left, you can copy that formula.

	A	B	C	D
1		January	February	Total
2	Sugar	6	5	=B2+D3
3	Chocolate chip	5	4	=B3+D4
4	Peanut butter	5	3	=B4+D5
5	Totals	=SUM(B2:B4)	=SUM(C2:C4)	=B5+D6
6				

Absolute Reference

But what if I don't want to use a relative reference? I want to add B1 to cells that are all over my spreadsheet.

	A	B	C	D	E	
1	Employee bonus	$100.00				
2				My salary	My salary with bonus	
3				$1,000.00		
4						
5	Joe's salary	Joe's salary with bonus				
6	$525.00					
7						
8				Mary's salary	Mary's salary with bonus	
9				$525.00		
10						

Let's say you need to enter a formula in cell B6 that will take the cell to the left and multiply it by B1 (cell 5 above). Then you want to be able to copy it to E3 and D9.

With relative referencing, you would enter = A6 + B1. But copying that formula to E3 and D9, doesn't work. Why?

Because by location, the cell to the left works ok (their salary is always to the left), but B1 is up 5 from my answer cell. What cell is up 5 from E3? Nothing. What cell is up 5 from D9? A blank cell.

So, we want to freeze B1 in our formula. To do this, we make B1 an absolute reference.

Try this formula in B6,

Calc = A6 + B1 (before pressing Enter, press Shift F4)

Excel = A6 + B1 (before pressing Enter, press F4)

Notice the dollar signs around B1; they instruct the software to use that specific cell.

Now you can copy that formula to E3 and D9 (Ctrl c and Ctrl v).

✔ Practice

Let's try one more example:

We want a formula in C2 to calculate the percent that 124 is of the total. So, our formula is

= B2/B7

	A	B	C
1		**Sales**	
2	Pie	124	
3	Pizza	95	
4	Pickles	687	
5	Popcorn	35	
6	Peanuts	19	
7	**Total Sales**	960	
8			

To be able to copy that formula down, we need to determine which number(s) are absolute references. The formula is taking the cell to the left (B2) divided by the total sales (B7). The total sales are the same, so that is our absolute reference.

Try this formula in C2:

Calc = B2/B7 (before pressing Enter, press Shift F4)

Excel = B2/B7 (before pressing Enter, press F4)

Now you can copy that formula to the range: C3:C6.

	A	B	C	
1		Sales		
2	Pie	124	12.92%	
3	Pizza	95	9.90%	
4	Pickles	687	71.56%	
5	Popcorn	35	3.65%	
6	Peanuts	19	1.98%	
7	Total Sales	960		
8				

Convert your numbers to percents.

To check your formula, see if the percentages add up to 100%.

What Is the Formula?

If you click on the Formula tab in Excel, you'll see several subcategories in the Function Library: Financial, Logical, Text, Date & Time, Lookup & Reference, Math & Trig, and More Functions.
Sometimes the trick is knowing which cells to use in the formulas. Let's go over a few of the most common ones.

Date & Time Functions

This is the easiest function to use, and a very important one. Often you need to insert a date in your worksheet. The most common use is probably inserting the current date and maybe even the time.

To do this, select any empty cell in your spreadsheet.

Formulas tab > Date & Time > NOW

	A	B
1	9/5/2009 16:01	
2		
3		
4		

Or you can use any of the other options to get to those selections:

f_x > Date & Time category > NOW function

Experiment with some of the selections in the Date & Time category. Notice how many of them are useful in working with payroll processes to determine employees' pay. For example, you can convert clock time to time based on 24 hours (military time).

Which is the most useful in your opinion? _____

Which is the least useful in your opinion? _____

Text Functions

The functions available in the text category affect text entered in a cell. For example, selecting LOWER will convert all of the letters to lowercase.

If you, for some reason, want a cell with numbers in it to be classified as TEXT instead of numbers, you can click on that, too.

For example, enter the following data. For cell B2, enter:

Formulas > Text category > Dollar > enter 500 for the first blank and 2 for the second blank.

	A	B	C	D	E	F	G	H	I
1		$ 100.00							
2		$500.00 ⟵							
3		$ 300.00							
4		$ 200.00							
5	Total	$ 600.00							
6									

Since B2 is text, the $500 isn't added into the total even though the formula calls for adding the range B1 to B4

✓ *Practice*

Experiment with some of the selections in the Text category.

Which is the most useful in your opinion? _____

Which is the least useful in your opinion? _____

Math & Trig Functions

Let's take an easy multiplication example:

If we sell 3 (A1) boxes of cookies for $5 (B1) each, to determine how much we make, multiply 3 by 5.

Various ways to enter the same formula:

a.   = A1*B1 (either type it in or click on it)

b.   = product(A1, B2) – notice that as you type the formula, help pops up to tell you to place commas between the cell locations

c.   Select [*fx*] (either the larger icon or the smaller one), for the Category, select Math & Trig > Product – the following dialog box pops up; you will click on A1 and B1 to indicate the location of the two cells to be multiplied

Function Arguments

PRODUCT

Number1 [   ] = number

Number2 [   ] = number

=

Multiplies all the numbers given as arguments.

Number1: number1,number2,... are 1 to 255 numbers, logical values, or text representations of numbers that you want to multiply.

Formula result =

Help on this function   [OK]   [Cancel]

d. Formulas > Math & Trig > Product – the same dialog box opens up.

The dialog boxes make it easy to use any formula as long as you know some of the terminology and the cell locations of the numbers to enter.

Round Function

The ROUND function is listed in the Math & Trig category. Or you can simply type the word "'round".

Using the round function to round numbers is useful, but it has an additional feature. The formula is =ROUND(whatever number you want rounded, the number of digits).

For example, if you just want the cell to round the number 65.8172 to 2 digits, you would use =ROUND(65.8172,2) {notice the comma}. The cell would display 65.82.

Or, if you want to calculate an answer and then round that answer, you would use

=ROUND(A1*B2,0)

If A1 is 4.512 and B2 is 54.123, the cell would display 244.

Roman Function

Another easy function to use is the Roman function. It converts a number to roman numerals. If the number 125 is entered in B3, and the function in B4 is =ROMAN(B3). Cell B4 will display CXXV.

 Practice

1. Practice using the Quotient function from the Math & Trig functions.

   a. What were your numbers? _____

   b. What was the formula? _____

   c. What was the answer? _____

2. Practice using the Round function on a cell that is the sum of two other cells. Begin with numbers with three digits after the decimal, round to one digit.

   a. What were your numbers? _____

   b. What was the formula? ? _____

   c. What was the answer? _____

3. Practice using the Roman function.

   a. What is the Roman numeral for 567? _____

   b. What is the Roman numeral for 1412? _____

   c. What is the Roman numeral for 980? _____

Financial Functions

Financial functions can get a little trickier, but they are good for everyone to be able to use.

Loan

Let's look at a loan, but before we create some formulas ourselves, we should look at a loan amortization template. See if you can open the following template. It may not be installed on your computer.

File > New > Install Templates > Loan Amortization > Create

Excel templates are pre-designed spreadsheets – all you have to do is enter the data.

	A	B	C	D
1	**Loan Amortization Schedule**			
3				
4				**Enter values**
5			Loan amount	
6			Annual interest rate	
7			Loan period in years	
8			Number of payments per year	
9			Start date of loan	
10			Optional extra payments	
11				
12		**Lender name:**		
13				

Enter the following data:

- Loan amount $25,000

- Annual interest rate 8% or .08

- Loan period in years 5

- Number of payments per year 12 [once a month]

- Start date of loan – today's date [##/##/####]

- Optional extra payments – leave this blank

Excel will calculate everything you need to know over on the right.

	Loan summary
Scheduled payment	$ 506.91
Scheduled number of payments	60
Actual number of payments	60
Total early payments	$ -
Total interest	$ 5,414.59

And the amortization schedule is calculated beneath that.

However, if you don't have the template, you may need to figure your loan payments yourself. With the same data, we'll use the PMT function.

Set up this blank spreadsheet:

	A	B	
1	Amount borrowed	25000	
2	Annual interest rate	0.08	
3	Number of years	5	
4			
5	Payment		
6			

Before we start entering the formula, notice that the template automatically determined the total number of payments by multiplying 5 years by 12 payments a year. The template also determined the monthly interest rate by dividing .08 by 12. So, we'll need to remember to do that in our formula.

In B5, enter the following either by typing or clicking on cells with the mouse; notice as you type that the software prompts you for the data (as long as you know what the abbreviations mean).

=PMT(B2/12,B3*12,−B1)

When you press Enter, your payment should be $506.91 (the same payment number the template calculated).

Let's look at each part of the formula:

PMT – you can also get to this by using ![fx] or Formulas > Financial > PMT

Financial ⌄		Date & Time ⌄	More Fun
ODDLPRICE	▲	brary	
ODDLYIELD		fx	
PMT		C	D
PPMT		PMT(rate,nper,pv,fv,type)	
PRICE		Calculates the payment for a loan based on constant payments and a constant interest rate.	
PRICE			
PRICE			
PV		ⓘ Press F1 for more help.	

If you didn't know it was PMT, you can always use Help or scroll through the functions and the explanations will be displayed.

B2 – this is our ANNUAL interest rate. Since the formula uses the monthly interest rate, we divide by 12

B3 – this is the number of years. Since we make a payment every month, we multiply this by 12

B1 – this is the amount we are borrowing. HOWEVER, our answer will be a negative number, which doesn't make sense. This means the bank would be paying us for borrowing their money! So, we need a negative number in here somewhere; this is an easy place for it.

Hopefully, if you got an unreasonable answer, you would be able to review your formula and fix any problems.

For example, if I didn't divide the interest rate by 12, my monthly payment would be $2,020! That can't be right.

Or, if I did divide the interest rate by 12 but I forgot to multiply the years by 12, my monthly payment would be $5,100! That can't be right.

Or, if I did both of these right, but forgot to make the last number negative, my monthly payment would be −$507. That would be great, but it can't be right.

 Practice

1. Think of a car you would like to buy and figure out the monthly payments using the formula if you borrowed for 5 years at 7% interest.

_____

2. Think of a house you would like to buy and figure out the monthly payments using the formula if you borrowed for 15 years at 6% interest.

_____

3. If you have a loan template, use it for the first practice exercise and see what the beginning balance would be in 2 1/2 years.

Lookup and Reference Functions

Let's look at an example of a lookup function.

We work at a bank approving loans. The interest rate we give people is based on their credit rating. The higher their rating (good), the lower the interest rate we will charge them (also good).

✔ *Practice*

Set up the following spreadsheet:

	A	B	C	D	E	F
1	Credit rating	Interest rate		Name	credit rating	interest rate
2	500	7.5%				
3	600	8.0%		Mr. Rich	752	
4	700	8.5%		Ms. Richer	693	
5	800	9.0%		Sonny Boy	1256	
6	900	9.5%		Sunny Girl	1351	
7	1000	10.0%				
8	1100	10.5%				
9	1200	11.0%				
10	1300	11.5%				
11	1400	12.0%				
12	1500	12.5%				
13	1600	13.0%				
14	1700	13.5%				
15	1800	14.0%				
16	1900	14.5%				
17	2000	15.0%				
18						

Ok, let's enter a lookup formula in F3 that will find Mr. Rich's credit rating in the table at the left and fill in his interest rate.

In F3, enter the following either with the mouse or keyboard:

=vlookup(E3,A2:B17,2)

When you press Enter, you should see that with a credit rating of 752, Mr. Rich's interest rate will be 8.5%.

The vertical lookup goes to a table (our range A2:b17) and looks up the value in the leftmost column.

The first reference in the () is the number we want it to look up, Mr. Rich's rating.

The second reference in the () is the range, which you can select with the mouse. Notice we don't include headings.

The next reference in the () is the column we want the answer to come from. I want the formula to look up the credit rating in the first column and pull the interest rate from column 2, so I enter a 2.

See if you can create the formula to determine Ms. Richer's interest rate based on her credit rating of 693.

Using Absolute Reference with a Lookup Formula

This is great and can save us a lot of time, but hopefully we have more than four customers at our bank. We really don't want to enter the formula for every customer, so we will use absolute referencing. Let's consider our original formula:

=vlookup(E3,A2:B17,2)

For absolute referencing, we have to determine what data will stay the same.

E3 – this is Mr. Rich's credit rating, but that won't be everyone's credit rating, so we cannot make that an absolute reference

A2:B17 – this is the table/array/range that we are looking things up in. It does stay the same for all customers, so we can make this an absolute reference.

After you select/highlight the entire range, press F4 and the formula will add $$ around both cell references: $A$2:$B$17

So, if we enter this formula in for Mr. Rich,

=VLOOKUP(E3,A2:$B$17,2)

We can copy/fill the same formula for the other customers.

 Practice

1. Let's see what our grade will be if we are using the following spreadsheet:

	A	B	C	D	E	F
1	Average	Grade		Name	Average	Grade
2	10	F				
3	15	F		Got it Smith	82	
4	20	F		Don't Get it Jones	61	
5	25	F		Lost Washington	50	
6	30	F		Straight A Nguyen	98	
7	35	F				
8	40	F				
9	45	F				
10	50	F				
11	55	F				
12	60	D				
13	65	D				
14	70	C				
15	75	C				
16	80	B				
17	85	B				
18	90	A				
19	95	A				
20	100	A+				

Enter a lookup formula to determine the grade for Got it Smith. Use absolute referencing so you can copy it down to the other three students.

> **Note:** *Notice that your array has to be in ascending order for the lookup to work.*

Logical Functions

Sometimes you want to use a formula that might have different answers based on what it finds in a cell. For example, if I'm preparing report cards for the grade spreadsheet we just finished, I might want to put a comment of "Great Job!" next to Straight A's and Got it's grades. But I might want to enter "Do your homework!" by Don't Get it's and Lost's grades.

The software can do this using an If function. There can be many different If functions. We will start with an easy one:

	A	B	C	
1	Customer	March Order	Customer ordered?	
2				
3	Mr. A	65		
4	Mr. B	14		
5	Mr. C			
6	Mr. D	35		
7	Mr. E	98		
8	Mr. F			
9				
10				

We want to enter a formula in C3 that will input "Yes" if the customer ordered in March and will leave the cell empty if he didn't order in March.

Enter this formula: =if(b3>0,"Yes","")

Note: *In a formula, if you are referencing a word or letter, put quotes around it.*

The parts of the formula:

=If – you can type this, or Formulas > Logical > If

B3>0 – The first item inside the () is what you are testing for, written as a formula, e.g., is a cell >, < or = another cell.

Then a comma

"Yes" – The second item inside the () is what you want to show in the cell if the test is true.

Then a comma

"" – The third item inside the () is what displays if the test is not true. We want the cell left blank, so "" leaves the cell blank.

Another way to create If formulas is to use the function wizard. Click on f_x . Select IF function, then click next.

Fill in the test, value if true, and value if false as shown in the picture, then click next.

Whichever method you use for entering the formula, it should generate this solution.

	A	B	C
1	Customer	March Order	Customer Ordered?
2			
3	Mr. A	65	Yes
4	Mr. B	14	Yes
5	Mr. C		
6	Mr. D	35	Yes
7	Mr. E	98	Yes
8	Mr. F		

Example 1

We own an appliance store and have five salespeople. We have the option to print a comment on their pay-checks every week. This week, for the salespeople who had 20 or more sales, the comment will be "Great job!". For the employees who didn't sell 20 or more, their comment will be "Good job!".

Set up the following spreadsheet. Create the If formula in C3 and copy it down before looking at the answer.

	A	B	C
1	Employee	Sales per month	Comment on paycheck
2			
3	1	14	
4	2	23	
5	3	71	
6	4	2	
7	5	13	
8			

Example 2

Now give the great employees a bonus of $100. Create an If formula in D3 that will give great employees $100 (don't enter the $), and good employees get $0. Copy the formula down to the other employees.

	A	B	C	D
1	Employee	Sales per month	Comment on paycheck	Bonus
2				
3	1	14	Good job!	
4	2	23	Great job!	
5	3	71	Great job!	
6	4	2	Good job!	
7	5	13	Good job!	
8				

Example 3

This one will be a little more difficult. Assume you have the following information: The boss has decided to give a 10% discount to customers who pay their bill on time at least 90% of the time. For customers who don't pay on time at least 90% of the time, display their original amount due.

Create the formula in D3 and copy it down. Hint: To determine the new amount for customers who get a discount, multiply the amount they owe by .9 (90%). Or, determine 10% by multiplying it by the amount they own and then subtract the 10% from the original amount.

	A	B	C	D
1	Customers	Amount due	Percent paid on time	New amount - discount
2				
3	Z	$524.82	95%	
4	Y	$6,514.23	86%	
5	X	$5,874.14	100%	
6	W	$2,136.24	100%	
7	V	$621.98	75%	
8				

Example 4

This is the most difficult of all because it involves an embedded if formula, which is an if formula inside an if formula.

Create the following spreadsheet:

	A	B	C
1	Students	Final Average	Grade
2			
3	Abe	72	
4	Al	94	
5	Andy	85	
6	Alex	98	
7	Antoine	77	
8			

There are three grades in this class:

$0 - 79 = C$

$80 - 89 = B$

$90 - 100 = A$

Create a formula in C3 to calculate the grades and copy it down.

Answers to Examples

Example 1 – C3=IF(B3>=20,"Great job!","Good job! ")

Example 2 – D3=IF(C3="Great job!",100,0)

Example 3 – D3=IF(C3>=90%,B3*.9,B3)

Example 4 – C3=IF(B3>90,"A",IF(B3>80, "B", "C"))

	A	B	C	D
1	Customers	Amount due	Percent paid on time	New amount - discount
2				
3	Z	$524.82	95%	$472.34
4	Y	$6,514.23	86%	$6,514.23
5	X	$5,874.14	100%	$5,286.73
6	W	$2,136.24	100%	$1,922.62
7	V	$621.98	75%	$621.98
8				

✔ Practice. Write If formulas for the following.

1. Create names and number grades for five students. For those that receive at least a 60, display "Passing"; for the rest, display "Failing".

2. Give a curve to some of the students in #1. For those over 89, add 3 points. For those not over 89, display "Thanks for taking the class".

3. Create names and order numbers for five customers. We are printing invoices (bills). On the invoice, we will print "Thanks for your business" for customers who ordered at least 100 cases of our ice cream. "Check out our new flavors" will print on all other invoices.

4. Determine a discount for customers who ordered at least 75 cases. For customers who qualify, determine what 5% of their order is. Do nothing for the other customers.

Multiple Sheets

Often you need more than one sheet in a workbook. A perfect example is a budget.

✔ Practice

Create the following budget spreadsheet:

	A	B	C	D	E
1	Budget				
2		January	February	March	Total
3	Revenue				
4	Sales	$1,756,842	$2,134,867	$1,025,462	$4,917,171
5	Interest Income	$12,054	$30,215	$9,541	$51,810
6	Total Revenue	$1,768,896	$2,165,082	$1,035,003	$4,968,981
7					
8	Expenditures				
9	Rent	$250,000	$250,000	$250,000	$750,000
10	Raw materials	$214,361	$154,398	$265,451	$634,210
11	Salaries	$412,062	$430,257	$397,521	$1,239,840
12	Benefits	$103,016	$107,564	$99,380	$309,960
13	Total Expenditures	$979,439	$942,219	$1,012,352	$2,934,010
14					
15	Profit (Loss)	$789,458	$1,222,863	$22,651	$2,034,971
16					

Profit = Total Revenue − Total Expenditures

Once we have the format set up, it saves time if we can copy it to another sheet.

Right click on the tab for Sheet 1 at the bottom of the budget sheet. Notice you can rename the tab, protect the sheet, and even change the color of the tab. But, what we are interested in is copying this sheet to Sheet 2. Select Move or Copy.

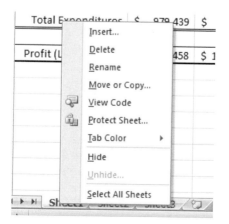

Select Sheet 2 to place our new sheet before Sheet 2. And check the box Create a copy.

You now have a second sheet exactly like the first. While you are at it, you can make two more copies so we have four budget sheets.

You can rename them by double-clicking on the sheet tab or right-clicking on it and selecting rename.

You can change the months on the 2nd, 3rd, and 4th quarters and you would need to change the numbers in each of the other budgets since it is unlikely your revenue and expenses are exactly the same every month.

To create a total sheet without retyping everything, copy one of the quarterly sheets to Sheet 5 and delete the columns you don't need, delete the numbers, and change the headings.

Sheet 5: Total Sheet

	A	B
1	Total Annual Revenue and Expenses	
2		Total
3	Revenue	
4	Sales	
5	Interest Income	
6	Total Revenue	$-
7		
8	Expenditures	
9	Rent	
10	Raw materials	
11	Salaries	
12	Benefits	
13	Total Expenditures	$-
14		
15	Profit (Loss)	$-
16		

Changing the Order of Sheets

The easiest way to move sheets is to click and drag the tabs. Release your finger when you reach the place where you want to move the sheet to.

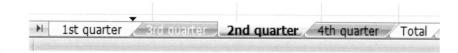

Cell Reference to Another Sheet

Since we want the fifth sheet to update automatically if anything changes in the other four sheets, we need to enter a formula for the totals.

Click on B4 and follow these directions (don't enter the commas):

= click on Sheet 1, cell E4, +, click on Sheet 2, cell E4, +, click on Sheet 3, cell E4, + click on Sheet 4, cell E4, ENTER

If you named the sheets the same way, this is the way the formula should look:

= '1st quarter'!E4+'2nd quarter'!E4+'3rd quarter'!E4+'4th quarter'!E4

Now you can copy this formula down to the other cells since all of the data are in the same order.

	A	B
1		Total Annual Revenue and Expenses
2		Total
3	Revenue	
4	Sales	='1st quarter'!E4+'2nd quarter'!E4+'3rd quarter'!E4+'4th quarter'!E4
5	Interest Income	='1st quarter'!E5+'2nd quarter'!E5+'3rd quarter'!E5+'4th quarter'!E5
6	Total Revenue	=SUM(B4:B5)
7		
8	Expenditures	
9	Rent	='1st quarter'!E9+'2nd quarter'!E9+'3rd quarter'!E9+'4th quarter'!E9
10	Raw materials	='1st quarter'!E10+'2nd quarter'!E10+'3rd quarter'!E10+'4th quarter'!E10
11	Salaries	='1st quarter'!E11+'2nd quarter'!E11+'3rd quarter'!E11+'4th quarter'!E11
12	Benefits	='1st quarter'!E12+'2nd quarter'!E12+'3rd quarter'!E12+'4th quarter'!E12
13	Total Expenditures	=SUM(B9:B12)
14		
15	Profit (Loss)	=B6-B13
16		

Formatting Multiple Sheets at the Same Time

Once you have several sheets set up, you might realize there were things you should have done on the original so that you wouldn't have to do it on each separately. For example, maybe you want all ten sheets to have the same footer.

To do this, Group them. Right-click on the tab for Sheet 1 and Select All Sheets. You'll notice it says [Group] after the filename at the top. Now, set up your footer or page setup however you like it. When you are ready to Ungroup the sheets, simply click on any of the other sheet tabs.

Book1 [Group] - Microsoft Excel

Review   View   Add Ins

Printing

It's important to get in the habit of previewing your spreadsheet before printing. It may take up several sheets and need to be formatted differently. Page setup offers several helpful features:

- Reduce or enlarge the spreadsheet.

- Select "fit to ___ page wide by ___ page tall" to control number of pages that print. This is a convenient way to make sure your spreadsheet fits on one page - just make sure you preview it to make sure it's not tiny and hard to read.

- Select gridlines to have cell lines print.

- Set row and/or column headings to print on each page; this is especially helpful with large spreadsheets.

- Print an entire workbook instead of printing each sheet individually.

Hiding and Unhiding Columns and Rows

If you don't want to delete rows or columns, but don't want them to show, use the Hide feature.

You can access it by right-clicking on the row number or column letter or by selecting Format in the Cells group on the Home tab.

Naming Ranges

Many people like to name cells or ranges to make it easier to apply formulas. For example, in the following spreadsheet, E6 can be named TotalRev.

	A	B	C	D	E
1	Budget				
2		January	February	March	Total
3	Revenue				
4	Sales	$1,756,842	$2,134,867	$1,025,462	$4,917,171
5	Interest Income	$12,054	$30,215	$9,541	$51,810
6	Total Revenue	$1,768,896	$2,165,082	$1,035,003	$4,968,981
7					

Then, in another cell that uses this total, when you start to type = TotalRev instead of clicking on the cell location, a prompt pops up so you can select it.

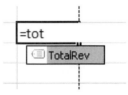

Range names must start with a letter or _. They cannot use hyphens or spaces.

Custom List

In the real world, you often end up typing some data over and over. For example, if I work for Shoe Universe and we have five locations, I would probably find myself entering these locations often. Excel allows you to create a custom list that will fill in the locations for you.

- Type the items on your list and select them

- Office Button > Excel Options > Popular

- Under Top options for working with Excel > Edit Custom Lists
- The cells you selected should be in the Import list from cells box > Import > OK > OK

To test it, on the worksheet, enter one of the items and drag over or down. Excel should fill in the other items from your list.

Sorting Data

It's easy to sort data—just make sure you keep all of the data together. For example, if I have a list of birthdays with each person's name and favorite cake flavor, I don't want to put the dates in order and mix up whose birthday it is and what kind of cake they like.

	A	B	C
1	Birthdays	Name	Cake
2	2/6/1984	Sister	Chocolate
3	6/14/1994	Brother	Strawberry
4	3/17/1965	Mom	Vanilla
5	3/18/1964	Dad	no cake
6			

To sort the data, select all of the data first (with or without the headings). Right-click and select Sort or select the Data tab and then sort.

Notice that there are various ways to sort. You can also sort by more than one column. For example, if I had many birthdays, I might list them first by date and then alphabetically by person within the dates.

Formulas

Thanks to the Internet, it is easy to find formulas if you don't know them. Here are a few common business formulas for reference.

- Price/Earnings ratio. If a stock costs $50 a share and has earnings of $2 a share, the P/E ratio is 50/2.
- Debt-to-equity ratio. This is total debt relative to outstanding shares. Use this to make sure a company doesn't have too much debt.
- Book Value. The book value of a company is all of its assets (building, cash, equipment, etc.) minus liabilities (debt).
- Assets = Liabilities + Equity.

Circular References

When working on a spreadsheet, you might have a message about a circular reference. This typically means that you have an error in your formula and you need your answer to get your answer. It can cause a loop that makes the problem unsolvable. Occasionally, for some reason, it may be necessary to leave a circular reference, but usually you need to correct them. Formula Auditing in Excel will help you find the circular reference and fix it. Or you can simply work through the formula to see what cells it is using and correct/change any cell references that are wrong.

 Projects

1. Ok. Time to become a millionaire. You just got your first real job. You are 22 years old and you decide to invest $100 every month. Use the future value formula to determine how much you would have 10, 20,

30, and 40 years from now. It should look similar to this, but, of course, you will format yours better. (Use absolute references when possible.)

	A	B	C	D	E	F
1	$100			Years		
2			10	20	30	40
3	Annual Interest Rate	2%	$13,272	$29,480	$49,273	$73,444
4		3%	$13,974	$32,830	$58,274	$92,606
5		4%	$14,725	$36,677	$69,405	$118,196
6		5%	$15,528	$41,103	$83,226	$152,602
7		6%	$16,388	$46,204	$100,452	$199,149
8		7%	$17,308	$52,093	$121,997	$262,481
9		8%	$18,295	$58,902	$149,036	$349,101
10						

2. Modify your spreadsheet for #1 – you decided to invest $150 from every paycheck (and you get paid twice a month).

3. For #2, how much would you have saved investing for 40 years at an 8% interest rate? How much had you paid in after 40 years (40 years, $150 twice a month)? This is the beauty of compounding interest—and the moral of the story is: start saving early and make it constant.

4. Now, see if you can find out how to use Count(if). Assume you have received 100 survey responses. One of the questions was a Yes or No answer. Create a spreadsheet with 1-100 in column A and randomly enter Y or N for each of them in column B. Using Help if necessary, create a Count(if) formula to determine how many people answered Yes.

5. Create a budget for yourself; the numbers can be imaginary. Make sure your budget has:

   a. A sheet for each of the four quarters and a total sheet

   b. At least two revenue categories

   c. At least five expense categories

   d. A chart of some type

6. Track the money you have in your bank account for three months on three separate sheets (the data can be made up).

   a. Make sure that the beginning balance for Sheets 2 and 3 is based on the ending balance of the prior sheet.

   b. Include at least three deposits each month.

   c. Include at least five withdrawals (checks, ATM, PayPal) each month.

   d. Make sure your ending monthly balance is always positive.

   e. Include clip art and a graph.

7. Prepare a payroll sheet for 10 employees.

   a. Include the following categories:

      i. Hourly rate

      ii. Hours worked

      iii. Gross pay

     iv.   Taxes (20% of gross pay)

     v.   Health coverage (select if they have family coverage or single coverage; have some of each)

     vi.   Insurance cost − $150 for family, $75 for single (use an IF formula for this)

     vii.   Net pay = gross pay − taxes − insurance cost

8. Create a workbook to track your grade point average.

    a. Sheet 1 will be your Freshman year in college.

    b. Sheets 2 through 4 are for Sophomore, Junior, Senior years.

    c. Each sheet should list classes taken (course code and name) and letter grade.

    d. Include a lookup formula for grade points (A = 4, B = 3, C = 2, D = 1).

    e. The total sheet should reference the other four sheets for the total grade points and total hours.

    f. Calculate GPA on the total sheet: GPA is the total points divided by the total hours taken.

DRAWING

STUDENT LEARNING OUTCOMES

After successfully completing this chapter, students will be able to:

1. Demonstrate the use of drawing software features to create images which have attractive formatting and fulfill their purpose.

There are many things you can do with drawing software. We'll look at a few basics using Windows Paint, OpenOffice.org Draw and Microsoft Visio. Since you've used so many different programs, it should be easy to figure out how to use drawing software. The main thing it takes is practice.

Changing a Photo Background with Windows Paint

There are easier ways to do this, but first let's experiment with the pixels. Find a photo you like (with a background other than white) and open it in Paint:

1. First, we'll erase the background – zoom to enlarge the photo.

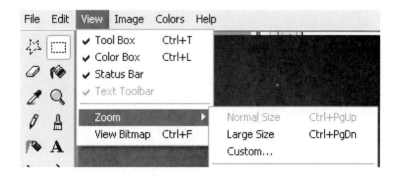

2. Using the eraser, erase the background, getting as close as you can without erasing the photo.

3. As a last step, use the Fill paint can to select a new background color or select a different background for your photo.

Creating an Ad with OpenOffice.org Draw

Some of the features of drawing programs include:

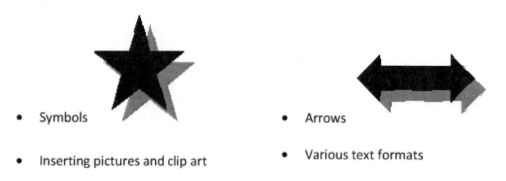

- Symbols

- Inserting pictures and clip art

- Arrows

- Various text formats

For people with imagination, drawing programs are perfect for creating marketing material.

✔ Project

1. Create an advertisement for a restaurant (real or imaginary). Make sure you include the name, address, and operating hours. Also, in your one-page ad, include at least one of the following:

    a. A background color {Format > Page > Background Tab > Select a color}

    b. A shape such as a rectangle with Text in it [T]

    c. A picture or clip art

    d. Symbols, lines, arrows, whatever you like to dress up your ad

    e. Bullets listing the chef's favorite dishes

Creating an Organizational Chart with Microsoft Visio

Visio offers many templates that make it simple to create drawings such as organizational charts.

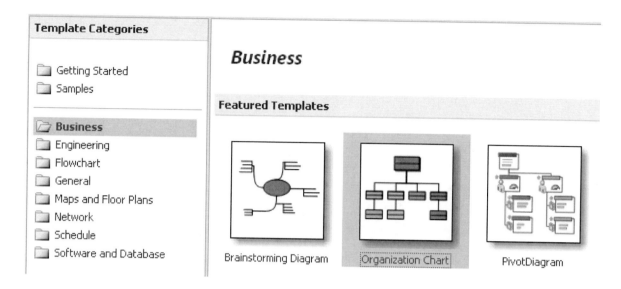

To add shapes to a chart, simply click on them on the left side and drag to the gridded section at the right. Shapes with a solid line show a direct chain of command. Some organizational charts show photos of the employees on the chart.

✔ *Project*

1. Create an organization chart for a company.

    a. You are the owner/manager.

    b. You have four departments. Name them whatever you like and put anyone in charge that you like (real or imaginary people).

    c. Each of the four departments has at least two employees working in them. Give them a title and list their names.

STUDENT LEARNING OUTCOMES

After successfully completing this chapter, students will be able to:

1. Demonstrate the use of a database to produce reports, query data, establish a relationship among tables, join tables to enforce referential integrity, and analyze data to solve business problems.

2. Design a database with efficient data retrieval and effective data security.

Information Technology helps businesses solve business problems. One of the main ways it does this is by providing information for decision making. All areas of a business need information. Assuming we make ice cream, here are some of the questions that reports can answer.

Question: What is our best selling ice cream?

Question: What ingredients do we need to order?

Question: Which employees are the most productive?

Question: How much would it cost if we gave all employees a 5% raise?

Question: Where should we build our new plant?

Question: How much money is available to invest in a five-year investment?

Databases are collections of data. The point of using databases is so that you can access what information you need when you need it. For example, you might have a list of data about your friends and family. Sometimes you might need their e-mail addresses, sometimes you might need their cell numbers, and sometimes you might need their birthdates. You would design your database so that it has all of that data and so that you can pull up just what you want when you want it.

Although you can make databases in most spreadsheet programs, to get a more powerful one with more database features, you will want to use a database program. Microsoft's database program is Access. OpenOffice.org's database program is called Base.

Most of the time, you will work with databases that already exist. You won't have to create one. But, it helps to learn how to design databases, and we need one to work with, so we'll design and create one.

First we'll talk about the parts of a databases. Databases are made up of tables, records, and fields. Think about a website selling music downloads.

- Fields – Their database will have fields that contain certain pieces of data about each song. For example, there will be a field for artist name (the singer or group), the title of the music, the type of music (rock, opera, alternative, etc.), the date, the price, maybe a short clip of the music, etc.

- Records – Each piece of music (each record) will have those fields even though one might be empty. For example, we may not have a music clip for every single song.

- Tables – A table will be made up of all of the records (one for each song).

So, it would look something like this.

Table – Songs for Sale
    Record 1 – song 123
        Artist name field – The Happy Players
        Song title field – We Are the Happy Singers
        Date field – January 2010
        Price field – $1.99
    Record 2 – song 124
        Artist name field – The Happy Players
        Song title field – Life is Good
        Date field – March 2010
        Price field – $1.99
    Record 3 – song 125
        Artist name field – Joe Washington
        Song title field – Life on Mars
        Date field – January 2010
        Price field – $1.99

There is an art to creating databases. Usually you want to have tables as small as possible. Normalizing a database involved creating several tables that are related—usually smaller tables with fewer columns instead of large tables with lots of columns. For example, you might have a separate table for each artist that is linked/related to a table of songs available for download.

We'll talk about relating databases later; first let's look at the fields.

There are some questions to answer when setting up the fields in the table. For example, how big does the field need to be? What kind of data is it (text, number, music clip, etc.)? Is it required? Setting up the fields correctly can prevent problems when the database is being used.

Field name	Kind of data	Size	Required?
Song#	Number		Yes
Artist	Text	75	Yes
Song	Text	100	Yes
Date	Date		Yes
Price	Currency		Yes

Tips:

- Identifying the type of data is important; you will want to think ahead. For example, you can identify zip codes as text, but if you ever want to find all of the zip codes that are > 77710 (for example), you need them to be a number.

- Think about what might be needed in the future. For example, we often sort large lists of names alphabetically by last name. Therefore, it wouldn't be a good idea to put the first name and last name in the same field—separating them makes it possible to sort by last name.

- Most database software sets the size default (automatic setting) fairly large. But, if it doesn't need to be that large, computer space is wasted. For example, in Access, text fields are automatically set for 255 characters. If you are creating a field for last name, you will probably never have a last name with 255 letters! So, set it as high as you think you will ever need it to be. You can change it later if you need to.

- Notice you don't have to set a size for currency, date, or number.

- Setting required fields as required ensures that they won't inadvertently be left blank. You have to assume a data entry person will be entering the data. To eliminate as many errors as possible, you set controls like 'required'.

✔ *Project*

You are going to design a database for family and friends. Some of the fields are identified for you, fill in the rest of the table and add two other fields you might want in the database:

Field name	Kind of data	Size	Required?
Last name			
First name			
Phone number			
Birthdate			

Primary Key – Another important thing to do when you are designing a database is to decide which field in a table is the primary key. A primary key is a field that is unique. For example, in your family/friend database, two people could have the same last name, so that can't be the primary key. Neither can first name, phone number, nor birthday, because you could have duplicates of any of those. You may not know people with the same birthday now, but remember you are building a database that you can add to, since you might know people with the same birthday in the future.

Usually, the primary key is a number assigned to each record. Before data security was such a big problem, we used to use social security numbers. Now we assign a new unique number— School ID number, customer ID number, etc.

So, in our family/friend database, we will add a number field. The database can automatically assign it or we can assign it.

Now we create our database.

Creating a Database

One thing that is different with databases is that you name the file at the very beginning.
In OpenOffice.org Base, you select "Create a new database" and you name it.

Access has several templates you can use, or you can create a new blank database.

Tables

The OpenOffice.org Base screen gives you these choices. The Wizard is very helpful, but since we are learning how to set up a database, we'll use "Create Table in Design View".

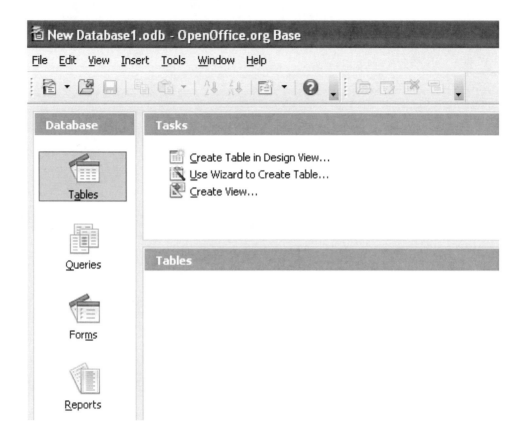

Access opens up in Datasheet view.

To switch to Design, click on View at the left or click on the little arrow below View and select Design.

The Base screen has columns for us to enter field name and field type and description. The description field is voluntary. If you think users may not know what the field name means, you can enter a text explanation. Notice that Required and Size are down at the bottom and the default size is 50 in Base.

The Access screen is similar, however there are more options at the bottom of the screen and the default field size is 255.

Practice

Enter your six fields. Designate the name, type, size, and whether or not the field is required. Also, add a primary key field (ID number). To designate this as a primary key in Base, right click and select Primary Key.

To designate it as a primary key in Access, select the row of the primary key and click on Primary Key. If you need to take the Primary Key designation off, just click on it again.

Now that the fields are set up, it's time to enter the data. First, save the table. You'll be asked to give it a name. Remember that this is a table, and we could have more than one table in a database.

Once you've saved the table, you can enter the data for your friends and family. Enter one friend per row.

 *Practice*

Enter data for 10 friends and/or family members. You can make up data if you like, this is just for practice.

LName	FName	ID number	Birthdate	City	State
Adams	Aaron	1	03/08/86	Houston	TX
Bush	Betty	2	08/23/84	Atlanta	GA
Cleveland	Curtis	3	05/05/85	Dallas	TX
Fillmore	Francis	4	11/04/86	Houston	TX
Grant	Gary	5	03/24/87	New York	NY
Harding	Hal	6	09/23/86	El Paso	TX
Eisenhower	Ernie	7	01/25/85	Dallas	TX
Kennedy	Keri	8	12/30/85	Brownsville	TX
Lincoln	Lakesha	9	07/07/87	Houston	TX
McKinley	Mickey	10	07/23/84	El Paso	TX

Great! You designed a database.

The great thing about having a database is that you can search for certain items, sort in different ways, and prepare a variety of reports.

Reports

Preparing reports is easy. Both Base and Access have a report wizard that has most of the common report features.

Base – Save the table and close it > Click on Reports > Use Wizard to Create Report

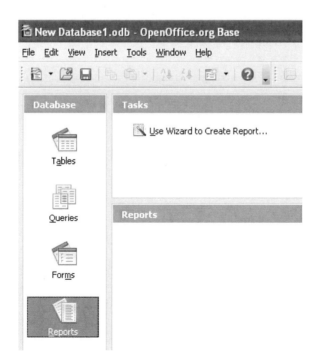

Access – Create Tab > Report Wizard

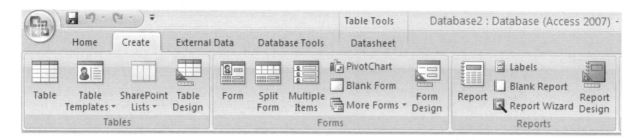

- Make sure the table you want to use is selected.
- Select the fields you want in your report by double-clicking on them or clicking on the ▷ arrow to put them in the box on the right.
- Click Next to experiment with some of the report options.

Report Wizard

Steps

1. Field selection
2. Labeling fields
3. Grouping
4. Sort options
5. Choose layout
6. Create report

Which fields do you want to have in your report?

Tables or queries

Table: Table1

Available fields

ID number
City
State

Fields in report

LName
FName
Birthdate

Binary fields cannot be displayed in the report.

| Help | < Back | Next > | Finish | Cancel |

Notice some of the choices for your report:

- Grouping
- Layout
- Adding a title
- Sorting

The following is an example of the report in Base.

	Author
	Alicen Flosi

Last Name	First Name	Birthdate
McKinley	Mickey	07/23/84
Bush	Betty	08/23/84
Eisenhower	Ernie	01/25/85
Cleveland	Curtis	05/05/85
Kennedy	Keri	12/30/85
Adams	Aaron	03/08/86

Queries

One of the main purposes for any database is to sort or pull out certain information, for example, a list of only the family or friends that live in Texas. This is done with a Query.

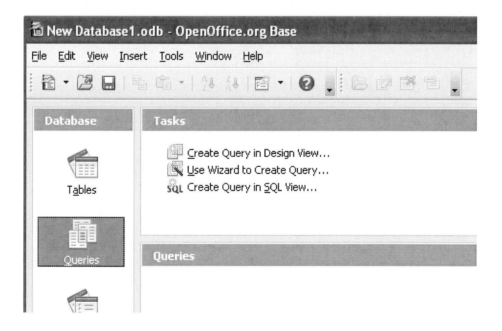

 *Practice*

Select query in Design View. Select your table. And add it then close the add Table box.

File	Edit	View	Insert	Tools	Window	Help

Add Table or Query

○ Tables   ○ Queries

☐ Table1

Add

Close

Help

Field			
Alias			
Table			
Sort			

Select the fields you want in the query: First Name, Last Name, and State by double-clicking on them. They will appear in the columns at the bottom.

File	Edit	View	Insert	Tools	Window	Help

Table1

```
*
LName
FName
🔑 ID number
Birthdate
City
State
```

Field	LName	FName	State
Alias			
Table	Table1	Table1	Table1
Sort			

If you have the same state for more than one person, use that state as your criterion. For example, we are looking for people in Texas. So, our criteria for the State field will be TX.

> **Note:** *The criterion has to be entered the same way as the data was entered in the table. Also, if you are searching for Texas and you entered it as TX in some places and Texas in other places, the results will only show those entered as Texas. This is a major problem with search engines; well, really the problem is with the people entering the data. Be consistent.*

OpenOffice – type in TX. Make sure it is in the State column.

Access – type = TX and the software will add ' or " if needed. Make sure it is in the State column.

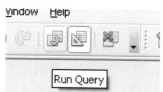

To run the query in OpenOffice.org Base, select . The results will display in a table form.

To run the query in Access, select ![Run] . The results will display in a new window.

Of course, to make the query look better, you can then make a report from it. The same way we created a report from our original table.

Forms

The fourth item in a database is a form. Forms make it easier to enter data, view data, and look through the records.

The form wizard works the same as the report wizard. Select the table or query that you want to use, select the fields in the form, and make other selections going through the steps. Using >> selects all fields.

Form Wizard

Steps

1. Field selection
2. Set up a subform
3. Add subform fields
4. Get joined fields
5. Arrange controls
6. Set data entry
7. Apply styles
8. Set name

Select the fields of your form

Tables or queries

Table: Table1

Available fields

LName
FName
ID number
Birthdate
City
State

>
>>
<
<<

Fields in the form

Binary fields are always listed and selectable from the left list.
If possible, they are interpreted as images.

Help   < Back   Next >   Finish   Cancel

Notice on the following form example by using the arrows at the bottom of the screen.

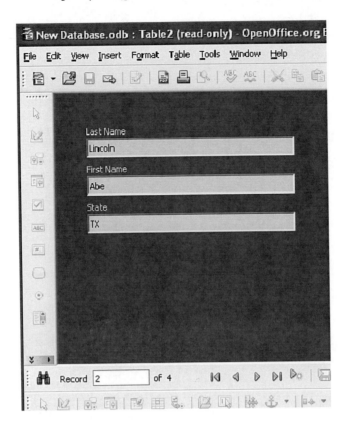

Validation Rules

Sometimes it is helpful to include validation rules in the design. These control what data can be entered in a specific field. For example:

- > 10
- = TX or LA
- = female or male
- = M or F

These help prevent data-entry error. For example, if you have 2 employees setting up a database of employees and one enters female or male for gender and the other enters M or F for gender, you would have a problem when it came time to prepare a report of males. Validation rules can also prevent general data entry mistakes.

To enter validation rules in Access, while you are in the Table Design, select the field that the rule applies to and enter the rule in the screen at the bottom. The following is for M or F. (If you type = M or F, the software will add the quotes because it is text.) The validation text below that line is the error message that will pop up on the screen if the user tries to enter something other than M or F. After entering the validation rule, try to enter a record that doesn't meet the criteria. The error message should pop up.

General	Lookup	
Field Size	1	
Format		
Input Mask		
Caption		
Default Value		
Validation Rule	="M" Or "F"	
Validation Text	Must be M or F	
Required	Yes	
Allow Zero Length	Yes	
Indexed	No	
Unicode Compression	Yes	
IME Mode	No Control	
IME Sentence Mode	None	
Smart Tags		

Lookup Columns

Lookup columns make it easy to enter data into tables. If you create a lookup column, for example of all of the states in the U.S., then when you are entering the data, you would just click on an arrow and pick the state off of a list.

To create a lookup column in Access in Table Design, select Lookup Wizard in Data Type for the field.

	Table1	
	Field Name	Data Type
🔑	ID	AutoNumber
	State	Text
	Phone number	
		Text
		Memo
		Number
		Date/Time
		Currency
		AutoNumber
		Yes/No
		OLE Object
		Hyperlink
		Attachment
		Lookup Wizard...

If the table already has the values in it, you can have the lookup find the values in the table or a query or you can type the choices in.

Lookup Wizard

What values do you want to see in your lookup column? Enter the number of columns you want in the list, and then type the values you want in each cell.

To adjust the width of a column, drag its right edge to the width you want, or double-click the right edge of the column heading to get the best fit.

Number of columns: 1

Col1
TX
LA
NY

Cancel   < Back   Next >   Finish

Now when you are entering records, you can click on the arrow and select the state.

ID	State	Phone numk
1	TX	
2	TX	
3	LA	
(New)	NY	

Input Mask

Another useful feature in Access is to set an input mask. For example, if you want phone numbers to be entered as (123) 555-1234, you can design an input make for the format. Pull the wizard up by clicking on the ... on the right side of the Input Mask row.

The wizard will lead you through up the setup process.

Relationships

If your database has more than one table, some of those tables are probably related. To create a relationship between two tables, you need to identify the field that links them. For example, if our company has two tables – one for data about our customers and one for data about all of the orders, we might want to link them so that we can generate a report to see what orders were made by which customer.

One field in the two table will be linked: The Customer ID field. Notice that it is the primary key in the Customer Table. The same field is a foreign key in the Orders Table.

practice.odb : Customer - OpenOffice.org Base:

File   Edit   View   Tools   Window   Help

	Field Name	Field Type	
🔑	ID	Integer [INTEGER]	
	Customer ID	Number [NUMERIC]	
	Customer FName	Text [VARCHAR]	
	Customer LName	Text [VARCHAR]	
	Address	Text [VARCHAR]	
	City	Text [VARCHAR]	
	State	Text [VARCHAR]	
▷	Zip Code	Number [NUMERIC]	

practice.odb : Orders - OpenOffice.org

File   Edit   View   Tools   Window   Help

	Field Name	Field Type
🔑	ID	Integer [INTEGER]
	Order ID	Number [NUMERIC]
	Price	Number [NUMERIC]
	Order Date	Date [DATE]
▷	Customer ID	Number [NUMERIC]

Once we create the relationship, we will be able to find all of the data about the customer (name, address, etc.) for each order without entering it all again into the Order Table.

To create a relationship, select the tab for Tools > Relationships. We only have 2 tables in our dbase and we want to link them, so click on the first one, then Add, then click on the second one and Add, then close the Show Table box.

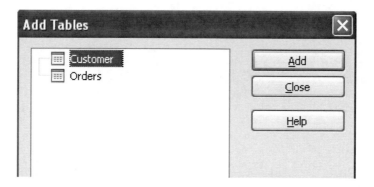

In Access, if you accidentally forget to add one or add one too many times, you can select Show Table or Hide Table to get rid of one or add one. Or right click in the black area of the relationships window and select Show Table. Or, right click in the blue bar by the Table name and Select Hide Table.

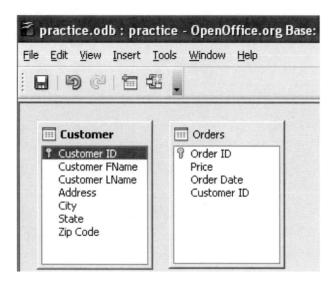

Now we will tell the software what the relationship is between the two tables. We are linking the Customer ID field in the two tables. Click on Customer ID in the Customers Table and drag it over and drop it on the Customer ID in the Orders table. Make sure you are linking the correct fields.

In Access, you will have the following choices:

- Enforce Referential Integrity – usually you will select this. This will make sure that any new orders in the Order Table will have Customer IDs that are valid in the Customer Table.

- Cascade Update. This will make sure that if you change a Customer ID number in the Customer Table, it will be changed in the related Orders.

- Cascade Delete. This will make sure that if you delete a Customer for some reason, any related Orders will be deleted, too.

Edit Relationships   ? X

Table/Query: Related Table/Query: Create

Customers ▼ Orders ▼   Cancel

Customer ID ▼	Customer ID	▲
		▼

Join Type..

Create New..

☐ Enforce Referential Integrity

☐ Cascade Update Related Fields

☐ Cascade Delete Related Records

Relationship Type: One-To-Many

Select all three: enforce integrity, cascade update, and cascade delete.

Notice the line connecting the two tables – it signifies a One-To-Many (one to infinity) relationship. One customer can have many orders, but each specific order is for only one customer.

One-to-Many relationship – one entity is related to many others. For example, a mother can have many biological children (theoretically), but a child can have only one biological mother. Also, you only have one birthdate, but many people can share the same birthdate.

Many-to-Many relationship – obviously, in this relationship, many entities are related to many others. For example, you can have many credit cards and those credit card companies can have many customers.

One-to-One relationship – one entity matches only one entity. For example, you have only one social security number (hopefully) and that social security number is owned by only one person. Same for fingerprints, retinas, etc.

Note:

- You cannot link two primary keys. If you had the same primary key in two tables, you should have just made one table with all of the data.
- The field you are linking needs to be the same type of data, i.e. text, number, etc.

Grouping

You can create reports that group data. For example, the following report groups employees by their hourly rate.

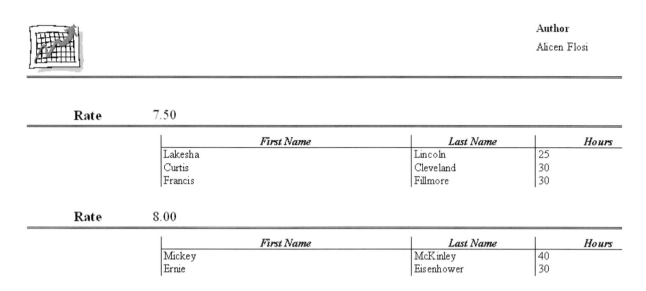

Author

Alicen Flosi

Rate	7.50		

First Name	*Last Name*	*Hours*
Lakesha	Lincoln	25
Curtis	Cleveland	30
Francis	Fillmore	30

Rate	8.00		

First Name	*Last Name*	*Hours*
Mickey	McKinley	40
Ernie	Eisenhower	30

Calculating a New Field

Another useful feature is calculating a new field. For example, if we want to create a field that multiplies hourly rate by the hours worked, in Access, follow these steps.

Create a new query in Design View. Select the fields you want. Right-click on the next empty field and select Zoom.

In the Zoom box that opens up, type the formula. First give your new field a name (Gross pay). Then enter a colon and the formula. Hours times Hourly Rate. Notice that the words inside the [ ] have to match the field names exactly.

Click OK. When you run the query, the new field will show the calculated results.

First Name	Last Name	Hours	Hourly Rate	Gross pay
Lakesha	Lincoln	25	$7.50	$187.50
Curtis	Cleveland	30	$7.50	$225.00
Francis	Fillmore	30	$7.50	$225.00
Mickey	McKinley	40	$8.00	$320.00
Ernie	Eisenhower	30	$8.00	$240.00
Gary	Grant	40	$8.50	$340.00
Aaron	Adams	40	$8.50	$340.00
Hal	Harding	35	$9.00	$315.00
Betty	Bush	40	$9.00	$360.00
Keri	Kennedy	25	$9.50	$237.50

You can also create a calculated field by selecting Build instead of Zoom. Build allows you to select the fields from a list instead of typing them in.

✓ Project

1. Set up a database with two tables.

   a.   Table 1 is a table of students at a university. It has the following fields (you can name it whatever you like):

      i.   Student ID Number

      ii. First Name

      iii. Last Name

      iv. Street Address

      v.   City

      vi.   State

     vii.   Zip

  b. Table 2 is a table of campus jobs. It has the following fields (you can name it whatever you like):

      i.   Job ID

     ii.   Job Title

    iii.   Hourly rate

    iv.   Hours per week

     v.   Supervisor

2. Create 10 students and enter their data in Table 1.

3. There are only three on-campus jobs – copier, ticket taker, and lab assistant. Add the data for each of those three records in Table 2.

4. Go back to Table 1 and add a field for job ID. Assign each of the 10 students to one of the three on-campus jobs.

5. Create the following queries:

  a. A list of the students who are ticket takers.

  b. A list of students and their hourly rates.

  c. A query that calculates their pay by multiplying hours times rate.

6. Create the following reports:

  a. A report of first names, last names, and city, sorted alphabetically by last name.

  b. A report of first names, last names, and position, grouped by position.

  c. A report from query (c).

7. List five management questions that could be answered by your database. i.e. Which three employees are the highest paid?

_____

_____

_____

_____

chapter 9

PRESENTATIONS

STUDENT LEARNING OUTCOMES

After successfully completing this chapter, students will be able to:

1. Create a slideshow which utilizes various features to share information on a topic.

2. Prepare a group presentation demonstrating the use of course concepts to solve problems in the workplace.

Slideshows can be attractive ways to share information. Using presentation software such as OpenOffice.org Presentation or Microsoft PowerPoint is the easiest way to prepare effective slideshows. The main rule for presentations is that you don't want to the slideshow to detract from the speech itself.

You can use a template—either one you downloaded or one installed with the software. The following pictures demonstrate the wizard in OpenOffice.org Presentation with an installed template.

- Keep it professional – there is a time and a place for pink backgrounds with white bunnies.

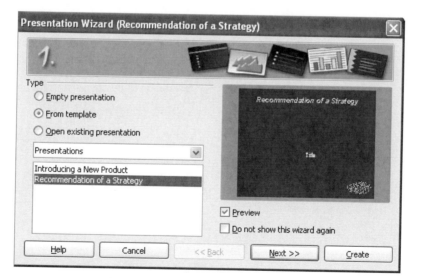

After you select a template, you can pick the background you like.

- Make sure you select a background that complements the presentation.

Then you can select the transition (the way you switch from slide to slide). You can also set the duration of the page and pause.

- Slide transition can really be annoying if it moves too slowly or is different for every slide. The goal is to have the audience listening to your speech, not waiting to see what slide transition is next.

If you want, the wizard can help you plan your presentation. First it will prompt you for an outline of your ideas.

Next, the wizard will take your ideas and suggest pages for the presentation.

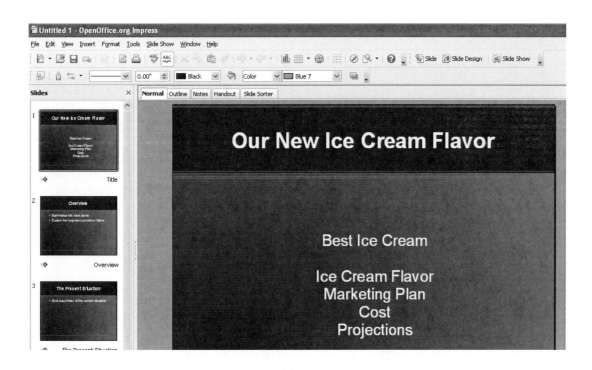

The resulting presentation will give you a skeleton to work from—you can modify, add, or delete slides.

Or, you can always create a slideshow without using the wizard or a template. Here are a few of the features.

New Slides

You can insert as many slides as you need. The slides can be title slides, slides with pictures, slides with graphs, etc. Select the layout.

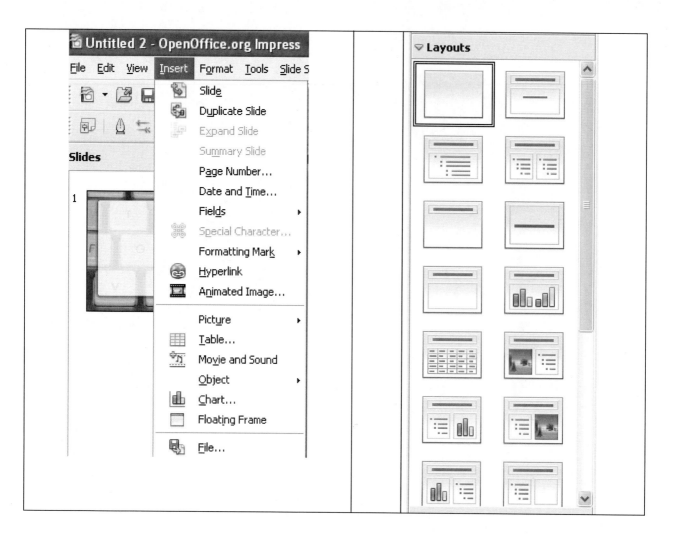

The animation and timings can be set through the Slide Show tab.

- If you set your slideshow to advance automatically, make sure you practice the timing several times. If you get distracted, add to your presentation, or get delayed by audience questions, your timed presentation will cause your presentation to look unprofessional. You may not have time to finish talking before it advances to the next slide. Or, you may finish talking and have to wait before it advances to the next slide.

PowerPoint

PowerPoint Options: You'll notice that many of the PowerPoint settings are similar to Word.

✓ Project

1. Slideshows should present the main points of a topic, not all of the information. For example, they should usually not have more than 6 or 7 bullets that are each not more than 6 or 7 words. Using the Internet, find five other tips for effective presentations.

    _____

    _____

    _____

    _____

    _____

2. Create a slideshow.

    a. Select one of the following topics.

        i. A not-for-profit organization

        ii. A proposal for solving one of society's problems

        iii. How to prepare an attractive, effective presentation

    b. Use the following features (on at least one slide).

        i. A picture or clip art

        ii. A table

        iii. A graph

iv.   Different fonts and sizes

v.   An appropriate theme or background

vi.   Slide transition

vii.   Animation

viii.   Other features as desired